BARNARDO CHILDREN IN CANADA

Gail H. Corbett

Barnardo Girls arrive in Canada. At left Miss Jennie Kennedy, Canadian-born staff matron holds smallest child. Circa 1900 —Centennial Museum, Peterborough

BARNARDO CHILDREN IN CANADA

Gail H. Corbett

Copyright © 1981 Gail H. Corbett
Illustrator: W. H. Chapman

Canadian Cataloguing in Publication Data

Corbett, Gail H.
    Barnardo children in Canada

ISBN 0-9690-751-0-3

1. Canada - Emigration and immigration - History.
2. Childrens-Canada - History. I. Title

FC548.I4C67   971.05   C81-094542-8
F1033.C67

Woodland Publishing, Peterborough
Box 2134, Peterborough, K9J 7Y4

Design - Suzanne Wood
Typesetting - Clay Publishing Co., Ltd.

Printed at Homestead Studios
Woodview, Ontario, Canada K0L 3E0

ACKNOWLEDGEMENTS

The Barnardo Children and their Descendants

Barnardo's of London
Mr. Clough
Miss Joynson

Centennial Museum, Peterborough, Ont.
Peterborough Public Library

City of Toronto, Archives
Ontario Archives

Manitoba Archives
Public Archives

Special thanks to all those who contributed in various ways to this book.

Dr. Roger Cardinal, Mr. William Astell, Mr. and Mrs. Harold Green, Mrs. Gordon Struthers, Mrs. Alice Griffin and Mrs. Daisy Peacock.

In particular to Bill, Reg and Andy who urged me on with their queries about the Barnardo Children in Canada.

LIST OF ILLUSTRATIONS

Distributing Home	Cover
Barnardo Girls	Frontispiece
Dr. Barnardo, Stepney Causeway	14
Girls' Village, Barkingside	17
Stepney Causeway and Babies' Castle	18
Parisian of the Allan Line	27
S. S. Sicilian	27
Barnardo Boys at Immigration Shed	32
Barnardo Trunk and Landing Card	32
Barnardo Special, Grand Trunk Line	36
Rural Canada	37
George Albertus Cox, A. de Brissac Owen	44
Miss Bessie Code and Hazelbrae	44
Marchmont Home, Belleville	49
Canadian Headquarters, Jarvis Street, Toronto	52
Mrs. Rose Hobday and older Barnardo Girls	52
Manitoba Cairn	58
Brown Roots	62
Edmund A. Struthers, Industrial Farm, Manitoba	71
Barnardo Homesteaders for Canada's West	71
Dr. Barnardo's Winnipeg Home	74
Road-making in Canada's Northwest, 1889	74
Miss Kennedy and new arrivals to Canada	84
Barnardo Girls at Hazelbrae, Peterborough	84
Dr. Barnardo's first Canadian Home	89
Garden Hill Station and Barnardo Children	94
Royal Albert Hall, London	94
Barnardo Boys at Work	103
Barnardo Girls as Mother's Helper	107
Dr. Barnardo's Home, Isle of Jersey	111
Barnardo Bugler and Gracie Fields	117
Watts Naval School	117
Map Canada	119
Farm Boys	134

CONTENTS

Acknowledgements
List of Illustrations
Preface

I   In the Beginning   11
II   Exodus   21
III O Canada   37
IV   Barnardo Children Go West   65
V   Barnardo Children Recall   77

Appendix   121
Bibliography   130
Index   132

PREFACE

Dear Reader,

The Barnardo Children In Canada is a portrait of children as pilgrims. It is a portrayal of the human spirit struggling against tragedy towards a new hope. It is the reflection of visionaries who believed in the potential of the individual and that rank was but the guinea's stamp. It is children building a better world for themselves and their descendants. It is the materialization of the hope that Canada promised to those who would journey.

Yesterday the children journeyed alone, seeking the promise of the New World. Today their numbers are legion and they are counted among our most courageous and successful nation builders.

Gail H. Corbett
Peterborough, 1981

DEDICATED
to

The Barnardo children in Canada
and
Their descendents,
to the
Men, Women and Children
who welcomed them,
to the
Spirit of the Visionaries
who believed in them
and to
Mable Bettes Ellis
who
sensitized my child's heart
to
"Nobody's Child"

PART I

Nobody's Child

Alone, in the dreary, pitiless street,
With my torn old dress and bare cold feet,
All day I wandered to and fro,
Hungry and shivering and nowhere to go;
The night's coming on in darkness and dread,
And the chill sleet beating upon my bare head;
Oh! why does the wind blow upon me so wild?
It is because I'm nobody's child?

Oh! what shall I do when the night comes down
In its terrible blackness all over the town?
Shall I lay me down 'neath the angry sky,
On the cold hard pavements alone to die?
When the beautiful children their prayers have said,
And mothers have tucked them up snugly in bed,
No dear mother ever upon me smiled–
Why is it, I wonder, that I'm nobody's child?

Phila H. Case, 1867

WHCHAPMAN.

IN THE
BEGINNING

". . . darkness was over the surface of the deep."

Genesis I

Out from under the dark waters of the Middle Ages a new industrialized England struggled to emerge. Feudal ties snapped, the masses fled the land, flocking to the great cities. The Industrial Revolution plummetted the nation into greatness and despair. London, the financial capital of the world, was rampant with unemployment. Masses of humanity sought to bury their despair in the cities' gin parlours, brothels and rat infested alleys. Families disintegrated. A fraternity of underworld children evolved: illiterate, furtive and desperate. Homeless children, scavenging for sustenance, sleuthed by day and shivered by night. Like Fagan's boys they formed their own underground. Thousands of "no-bodies' children" trembled in the black, back allies of the world's wealthiest nation. A philosophy of greed, propagated by an insensitive government and nurtured by the Church shackled the common people. Poverty and illiteracy raged. Charity schools received less revenue than the annual stipends of aristocrats' sons. Psychological, emotional and physical exploitation of children and adults perpetuated the poverty cycle which continued to turn the tread mill of man's inhumanity to man.

Dr. Thomas Barnardo at Stepney Causeway, charting out child emigration to Canada
Mrs. Frost Collection—Centennial Museum, Peterborough

In the late 18th century the human spirit sickened of injustices, bestiality, oppression and inequalities. The Evangelical and Humanitarian movements swept like prairie fires across the British Isles. The philantrophic movement was born, shining light into caves of despair, making paths straight in the wilderness, creating Ragged Schools, free hospitals, missions, Y.M.C.A.'s and Y.W.C.A.'s, creche systems and child welfare units. This marked the beginning of the great awakening of social conscience.

At this time, a young Irishman rose to become the greatest "Child Emancipator" in history. Through him, thousands of children were rooted in the great emerging nation, Canada.

Thomas John Barnardo was born on July 4th, 1845, of a devout Quaker family long resident as merchants in Dublin. Young Tom, the last and ninth child, was a voracious reader of Voltaire, Rousseau and Paine and early declared himself Agnostic. By sixteen, contrary to his family's wishes, he had abandoned his formal schooling, seeking his way in a business post at which he proved very capable but found personally unfulfilling. Intellectually intrigued but emotionally hostile towards the Evangelistic Revival sweeping the British Isles, Thomas reluctantly succumbed to an invitation to hear an address by the great tragedian John Hamilton. Barnardo was converted from scoffer to Evangelist and was imbued with the spirit that had fired John Wesley and had propelled the great British parliamentarian, Lord Shaftesbury.

In 1886 Barnardo entered the London Medical School determined to prepare for the Foreign Mission Field. However, the cholera epidemic broke. Barnardo served as a volunteer medic in East London where he discovered human miseries never imagined. Overwhelmed with the needs of the illiterate poor, the young Barnardo evangelized on street corners, compelling adults and children into his Ragged School which he had set up in an abandoned donkey shed.

One night, as Barnardo prepared to lock his school, he spotted a tiny figure crouched behind the heater. It was a boy in rags. Barnardo accosted him sharply:

> "Wake up! Off to your mother! You've nearly been locked in this place overnight!"
> The face of the boy was white with fatigue and hunger.
> "Well, that would suit me fine, sire! I ain't got no mother."
> "Well then off to your father."
> "Got no father neither, sir!"
> "Away, then, to your home, where ever it is!"
> "Oi've got no home, sir."
> "Are there more like you?" he asked the trembling lad.
> "Oh, yes sir!"

Barnardo followed young Jamie Jarvis through London's back alleys. To his horror, he discovered a "lay" where children's faces, aged with cold and hunger, bore witness to the untold miseries of child life. These were children untouched by Lord Shaftesbury's great Ragged Schools.

Shocked by this discovery, Barnardo accepted an invitation to address a large foreign mission rally being held in London's great Agricultural Hall. The next morning London's newspapers headlined the startling discovery of children struggling for existence in the core of the great metropolis.

"The Grand Old Man of Social Reform," Lord Shaftesbury, was shocked. He ordered the young radical to prove his story. At night, Barnardo lead this prominent parliamentarian and his wealthy associates into an army of destitute children. As Shaftesbury turned to leave he said to the young medic:

> "It may be that God is calling you to labour as his chosen missionary among the homeless children of this metropolis. The whole of London shall know about this."

Thomas Barnardo had found his mission. He successfully publicized his concern for homeless children and established the East End Juvenile Mission attracting hundreds of destitute children. By 1870 Barnardo purchased Stepney Causeway, a large building in East London close to the central railway. This Barnardo Home had a "mother and father" who boarded and trained about sixty destitute boys until employment or foster homes were secured. Admission to the Home was limited until the tragic death of "Carrots," a young boy, who had begged entrance, bed and board. But he was refused because he had employment as a match seller and his mother was alive. A few days later he was found under a bridge, dead from exposure.

In spite of financial problems, Barnardo determined never to turn away any needy child. The Barnardo Home motto was hung above Stepney Causeway:

> "No Destitute Child Ever Refused."

Although Barnardo was sensitive to the problems faced by homeless girls, his rescue work among female children posed problems for a bachelor. *How I Stole Two Girls* and *How I Fished For And Caught Her,* recorded some of his misadventures. In 1873 Barnardo married Syrie Louise Elmslie, and as a wedding present received "Mossford Lodge." This was their home and the nucleus for their rescue work among homeless and destitute girls. On July 9th, 1875, Earl Cairns, the British Lord Chancellor and first President of the Barnardo Board, officially opened the Girls' Village Home, Ilford, Essex.

Girls' Village Home, Ilford, Essex

Mrs. Frost Collection—Centennial Museum, Peterborough

The village was a world in itself with numerous cottages and "mothers," a school, a children's church, and a hospital. The children cared for their own cottage and were given instructions in the rudiments of learning and domestic science. Younger girls were placed in foster situations until Barnardo commenced his emigration programme.

In 1879, Teighmore House, near Gorey on the Island of Jersey was donated to Barnardo for little boys. A large main building, a church, gardens, hospital, headmaster, matrons, a gardener and a cook completed the Barnardo staff. The boys swam in Grauville Bay and played on the private beach. They were shipped to Stepney Causeway for emigration.

In 1881 Barnardo established a Labour House for young men who were unemployed and a young women's hostel. In 1884 Babies Castle, Hawkhurst, admitted a growing number of abandoned and destitute infants. Barnardo Youth and Infants from both these Barnardo Homes were to be emigrated to the Dominion of Canada.

Stepney Causeway, London: the great "Export Emporium"
— Barnardo Archives

Babies' Castle, Hawkhurst   — courtesy Mrs. Alice Griffin

ADMISSION TO BARNARDO HOME

"I want a man with no relatives and no schooling,
a man who would be out of the running altogether,
if he were not a strong man. And I cannot find
him. Every blessed foundling nowadays is snapped
up in his infancy by Barnardo Homes. . . . ."

Bernard Shaw.

In the early days of his work, many of Barnardo's proteges were "street-arabs," homeless boys and girls without trace of kin or friend. Later, most of the children were admitted reluctantly by widows, widowers or relatives in stringent economic situations. Each child admitted to Stepney Causeway was photographed in "before" and "after" clothing. An official admission record was completed, recording the condition and reason for admittance. Progress reports on the child were tabulated at intervals.

Here is a sampling of children and conditions to admittance as recorded by Dr. Barnardo.

Child Abuse

"R.P. (7) a poor maimed little fellow from a wretched Scottish town. . . had been brutally kicked and severely injured. Both parents degraded and living apart."

Death

"O.N. (11) Both parents died of consumption within a few weeks . . . he and two sisters (also admitted) left utterly destitute."

Widow

"E.F. (16) Applied for admission, ragged and shoeless. Mother left a widow with six children. Two of the little girls sold matches in the streets, and the boy carried parcels. The mother got an occasional day's charing. Family in a state of most pitiful poverty, and often on the brink of starvation."

Orphan

"D.J. (16) A raw country lad who worked on a canal bridge, but who lost his employment and took to a wandering life, finally making his way to London, where for a time he lived on the streets. Both parents dead."

Barnardo's "ever-open door" policy continued to attract thousands. Within ten years of operation the Barnardo Homes were receiving and caring for more children than any other agency in England. At first Barnardo was able to train his proteges in the domestics and trades and secure employment for them in Britain. But soon there were fewer and fewer employment situtations for his graduates and each year thousands of children poured through his "Ever-Open Door."

In 1889, Dr. Barnardo wrote of his concerns:

> "Of what avail is the rescue and training of young children, if we cannot find a sphere for their lives a sphere where, in their own most frequent expression, they can 'have chance?' Even in the very early days of my work it was plain to me that there was a danger of failure from my very successes. To be a life-giving force and centre of usefulness, the lake must have its outlets as well as its tributaries. The waifs and strays are ever growing up and new generations of equal misery taking their places.
>
> "My children too, were, by the very fact of their residence in the Homes, those who had in one way or another been 'pushed out of the running.' What was needed in order to give them the opportunity they had missed was in every real sense, a new heaven and a new earth, the fresh conditions of a colonial life."

PART II

"Through the night of doubt and sorrow,
Onward goes the pilgrim band
Singing songs of expectation,
Marching to the Promised Land."

Gould

WHCHAPMAN

EXODUS

As early as 1825 the concept of emigrating homeless children from Britain into Canada was advanced by Honourable Peter Robinson and the Rev. Thomas Socket, both of whom suggested that destitute children be emigrated to Canada as agricultural labourers. By 1830 the Children's Friend Society, London emigrated children into Lower and Upper Canada and distributed them to farms between Montreal and Niagara. In 1835, the *Cobourg Star* reported that the Society's Cobourg Committee had been set up, composed of leading citizens including the Rev. Bethune and Y. Burnham. The object of the Society was to place destitute British Children in Upper Canada where they were in great demand by British gentry attempting to establish agricultural units. In 1837 child emigration into Canada was terminated due to the Rebellions. However, by 1850, Lord Shaftsbury encouraged the exportation of pauper children to Canada to relieve the overcrowded cities. In 1853, Colonel Samuel Strickland, brother of the famed literary sisters, Susanna Moodie and Catharine Parr Traill stated in *Twenty-Seven Years in Canada West:*

"In towns and cities, educate the infant pauper population for emigration. Ragged schools in cities ought to supply us with these instructed in the arts we need. In the country, every house of industry should have a piece of land for spade husbandry, and a small farm for more extensive agricultural employment.

"Government should have ships and commissioners expressly for the purpose. Care should be taken of these children on the voyage and on their way up the country. Good masters and mistresses should be sought for them, and inquiries and visits occasionally paid them by persons appointed for the purpose.

"Regular depots should be formed in such towns as Montreal, Quebec, Kingston, Toronto and other places, under matrons and governors, for transmission to families requiring their aid; and little fear need be entertained of the kind treatment of these apprentices, in whose behalf, it should be enacted that they should not go away empty-handed from their three years' bondage, but should receive a certain sum in money, stock, or goods."

By the 1860's backed by the British government and propelled by the crying need for agricultural labourers in Canada, Maria Rye, feminist and Annie MacPherson, Quaker, headed child emigration into Canada. By the 1880's numerous child emigration agencies had surfaced including Mr. Fegan's Homes, Middlemore Homes, National Children's Homes and others.

Thomas Barnardo was hesitant about entering areas already overcrowded with child emigrant enthusiasts. He studied the negative report issued by Inspector Doyle on emigration of children into Canada and was sensitive to accusations that Great Britain's "street urchins" were being "dumped" on Canada's "virgin soil."

The fact remained: Canada needed young emigrants to serve on the land and Britain's cities were over-populated. In 1889, Barnardo recorded:

"We in England, with our 470 inhabitants to the
square mile, were choking, elbowing, starving each
other in the struggle for existence: the British colonies
over seas were crying out for men to till their lands,
with few ties to bind them to the mother country, and
at an age when they were easily adaptable to almost
any climatic extremes."

Barnardo was convinced that child emigration was essential. He
proceeded with caution.

"At first only by ones and twos and driblets, my
best boys and girls were scattered abroad over wide
sea and land, as opportunity afforded, to Australia,
New Zealand, to South Africa, to the European Continent, to the United States, to Canada. In this way
a small leakage of emigrants yearly, helped to relieve
the pressure from within the Mother Home, and to
keep the door open to further applicants. It was cer-
tainly good for us at home to find an open and honourable door by which the children could be sent
forth into life."

In 1868 he enrolled some of his Barnardo boys, including
Jamie Jarvis his first "street-arab", in Miss Annie MacPherson's
Canadian party. Anxiously, he awaited word of their Canadian
reception. Miss MacPherson penned:

"You will be glad to hear that all your boys seem
to have got comfortable places. This is a very fine
country with splendid openings for those who will
put their hands to anything for the first six months."

Canadian immigration inspector Mr. Louis Stafford, announced
that "Canada could do with a number of these lads."

Each year Barnardo enlarged his stream of emigrants until the
autumn of 1882, when he determined to launch a comprehensive
scale for the emigration of Barnardo Children into Canada.

The first shipload of Barnardo boys was prepared by the Rev.
Fielding, Governor of Stepney Causeway. He recalled, "At the
request of Dr. Barnardo, I selected fifty lads, outfitted them, went
to Liverpool and made full arrangements for their passage. . . "

The party consisted of boys between the ages of fourteen and seventeen, of these, thirty-one were orphans, thirteen had living mothers, five had fathers only, five had destitute grandparents and eleven had no friends. On August 10th, 1882, Dr. Barnardo sent off his first party of Barnardo boys aboard the Parisian and prayed for their welfare and success in the New World.

On reaching Canada, the Barnardo party travelled to Hamilton where a distributing Home placed them out within a fortnight. In 1883, a second party of Barnardo boys landed in Canada; they were inspected by Federal and Provincial agents and distributed into rural districts of Ontario.

By 1883 Dr. Thomas Barnardo was convinced that:

> "Well-planned and wisely conducted child-emigration especially to Canada, contains within its bosom the truest solution of some of the mother country's most perplexing problems, and the supply of our Colonies' most urgent needs. . . First, it relieves the over-crowded centres of city life and the congested labour markets. Second, it supplies what the colonies are most in want of, an increase of the English speaking population. Third, it confers upon the children themselves unspeakable blessings. The change at the young and formative period of their lives gives to each child whose character is good, and who is successfully absorbed into the colonial population, such an immediate prospect of an independent existence upon a higher plain as hardly could have been imagined as within its reach."

Determined to conduct a successful programme Barnardo drew up the following:

EMIGRATION PRINCIPLES

I   CANADA
   was to be the principal direction of emigration because it was the nearest British colony; the journey was short and inexpensive; the weather was admirable and the demand for settlers was insatiable.

Barnardo Children on board the S.S. Sicilian, March 11th,
1920 — *Barnardo Archives*

The emigration ship Parisian , Allan Line docked in Mon-
treal harbour having unloaded hundreds of Barnardo chil-
dren — *Public Archives of Canada*

II. CHARACTER:
Only the "flower of the flock" would be emigrated. They should be honest, industrious and capable; taught to revere the Bible as God's word; free from taint.

III. PHYSIQUE:
Each child was to be thoroughly sound and healthy of body with no predisposition to disease; no disablement in limb and no failure of intellect.

IV. ACQUIREMENTS:
The Barnardo Child was to have the rudiments of a plain English education; the boys trained in agricultural or industrial pursuits, the girls in domestic science.

V. GUARANTEES:
Barnardo promised systematic visitation and regular correspondence with the young emigrant; in case of moral failure the Barnardo child would be returned to England at Barnardo's expense.

Barnardo's emigration programme gained momentum. The "cream of the crop" sailed for Canada. Annually thousands of children were herded from destitute and dead-end environments and assembled "en masse" at Stepney Causeway, the great Export Emporium.

In 1912 the Governor of Stepney Causeway wrote concerning emigration of Barnardo Children to Canada:

> "For many years dear old dingy Stepney has been your Central Store, your Wholesale Warehouse, your Export Emporium. We have never sent you all you asked for. (I verily believe you would bankrupt the British Empire by your demands!) You have had our finest boys—fellows that it half broke our hearts to part with, whose absence desolated the ships and saddened the playground and took the pith out of our dormitory matches and pillow fights. You have also had our 'pickles': good chaps, we grant you, but over-endowed with boyish spirits. Perhaps we have not been so sorry to part with these. But they are just the sort of emigrants—pushful, stirring, optimistic, rough and ready—that you most gladly welcome, and while we

do not exactly weep at their going we know they will
do us credit when you get them into your clutches.
We have sent you our lads by the hundred and by the
thousand, and even while we rejoiced in the great
future that you offered them, we saw them go with
regret.

So let me say in all frankness, that Canada in
Stepney Causeway, as well as in the Girls' Village
Home, is not to many of us the bright and joyous
word that you would fain paint it. Your Canada
parties break across all our Home life. The school-
master laments his cleverest pupils, the shop masters
lose their top boys, every office wonders where it
will find a messenger as good as the last, and all
because of the detestable 'Canada List'!"

The "Canada List"

Children qualifying for the "Canada List" were assembled at
Stepney Causeway where they were tested, lectured and outfitted
for the "great Canadian Adventure". Any defect and the child
was scratched from the list.

Louisa recalled: "My sister and I were picked to go to Canada
to-gether but they found something wrong with her eye. They
wouldn't let her come with me. My heart was broken."

One child remembered having her tonsils removed before
qualifying for the "Canada List."

"I was to have my tonsils removed. They set me in a chair in
the children's hospital, and out came my tonsils. Now, I was ready
for Canada!"

Sometimes children recalled embarrassing moments. Albert
stated: "We were taken to Stepney Causeway where about forty
of us boys were asked to strip naked and march past the doctor.
I remember how humiliated I was when the doctor called the nurse
to come and have a look, and them laughing at our nakedness."

Once the medical was passed, the child was supplied with his
"Canadian Outfit" packed in the Barnardo trunk. This trunk man-
ufactured at the Barnardo Technical School was constructed of
hardwood and covered in imitation alligator skin. It contained a
Bible, with the date of emigration, a Sankey Hymn Book, Pilgrim's

Progress, and the Traveller's Guide. Clothing was made at homes of industry showing the ear-mark of British excellence. Barnardo Children were among the best dressed emigrants to enter Canada. Each Barnardo Child carried a personal travel bag, his Barnardo number, destination and landing card. The "flower of the flock" was assembled. Canada lectures and agricultural slides were presented. The children were challenged with the great future awaiting those who worked hard in the Dominion of Canada.

THE GREAT DEPARTURE DATE

Canada banners flying, the Barnardo Band blaring, the children marched two by two through London Streets leaving Stepney Causeway and the Girls' Village. Travel bags in hand they boarded the "Barnardo Special", which whisked them and their escorts, usually a Royal Patron, Dr. Barnardo and staff members, toward the emigration docks at Liverpool.

The sight of several hundred children leaving for over-seas affected individuals in various ways. One Barnardo Girl remembered a woman, whom she presumed to be her mother, press a small container of warm cream into her hand. Sometimes, there seemed to be a feeling of pity. One man was seen sobbing profusely as the train pulled out. Someone standing near suggested that there was nothing to cry about for the children were leaving for a good country and were very fortunate to be going there.

Until his death Dr. Barnardo accompanied each emigration party to the departure docks. He wrote of his sincere concern for his "little pilgrims."

> "My heart cries out within me, nor can any words
> which I can now utter express my feeling. All I
> could do on Monday, Tuesday, Wednesday, and
> Thursday was to cry to God for help on behalf of
> my dear children who have gone out to Canada
> without my seeing them, or praying with them, or
> giving them my blessings. . . . Poor little darlings!
> I hope all has gone well with them. I long to get
> a report from you, however brief. Yet, the feeling
> that these are now divided from me, perhaps for
> ever, that I may never see them on earth, and have
> not bid them good-bye, is a sore pang in the remembrance."

At the time of Dr. Barnardo's death in 1905 — 18,172 Barnardo Boys and Girls had been sent to Canada.

"CANADA CLAUSE"

Within the first few years of Barnardo's emigration programme to Canada, a wave of litigation forced Barnardo to admit that he had emigrated some children into Canada without parental consent. In 1888 the Poor Law Act was revised to state that in cases of deserted children parental rights and obligations were transferred to the guardians of the parish. Two years later the Custody of the Children's Act, popularly referred to as the "Barnardo Act", stated that boards of guardians were permitted to send children to the colonies without the consent of the parents. By 1892 each admission to a Barnardo Home was accompanied by the signing of this clause.

The "Canada Clause" was not popular. The following is a letter from a Barnardo Girl in England to her brother, a Barnardo Boy in Canada:

Dear Harold,

Mother died of a broken heart. That is straight from the doctor's mouth. You may think I am a bitter woman but I will never forget or forgive the people responsible for it. She tried for years to get us all back with her, but no, they parted us all and it need not have happened. They wouldn't let us go home to her while she was alive. . . it's as bitter as gall to me.

Love, your sister.

If Barnardo suspected that the child's parent was hostile to the "Canada Clause" the child was not permitted to correspond with his family before emigration. Barnardo's "After-Sailing" notices were forwarded once the child had landed in Canada.

The Barnardo home did encourage the young settlers to assist in the emigration of their parent(s) and relatives to Canada, once they had earned enough on the Canadian farm. The 1903 *Ups and Downs* reported that "each time we go over we carry a big list of mothers, sisters and brothers of boys in Canada whom we are commissioned to hunt up and bring out at the expense of the boys, who provide the necessary funds from their savings."

Barnardo Boys at the Immigration Sheds, New Brunswick
— Public Archives, Ottawa

Barnardo Trunk with the Canadian Outfit

Landing Card: Harold Green, Age 13   S.S. Melita, St. John's, New Brunswick, 1923

—Photo William Astell, Peterborough

ALL ABOARD FOR CANADA!

By the 1900's Barnardo Children filled the steerage compartments of Britain's major steamships. The Allan Line was regarded as part and parcel of the Barnardo emigration machinery. The most popular ships were the Corinthian , the Sardinian , the Sicilian , the Melita , the Parisian and the Tunisian . Besides a few passengers, the ships could transport up to 400 children at one crossing. Four parties of children sailed each year. The total cost from London to Canada was less than one year's boarding-out in England.

Barnardo staff usually included one medical personnel, some of whom were travelling trans-Atlantic for the first time. A nurse who was later to serve as a Lady Visitor reported:

> "This was my first trip across the Atlantic. No doubt I took a gloomy view of things, for the sea treated me so badly. But I was not alone in my misery: several of our young friends kept me company in a very manly way."

Sea-sickness was a major complaint among the children. It was Barnardo's policy that they were "doing a boy a good turn who lying inanimate and thinking he is going to die, make him get up, stand to attention, go through several smart evolutions, march down two flight of steps, sing grace and take his tea at the table."

Each Barnardo staff was requested to record the voyage for the Barnardo publications *Nights and Days* and *Ups and Downs*. Nurse Viscink wrote:

> "There were the same orders, day after day, at six a.m. 'All out!' And then the long washing process, when every boy comes shuffling along, stripping as he comes, ready to get into the wash house.
>
> "A certain crowd of sick laddies press round the small compartment known as 'Nurse's Medicine Shop,' with loose or blackened bandages or some ailment to be treated.
>
> "A little later the lining up on deck's ready to file down for breakfast. How often, when the sea seemed rough, that line has seemed endless, and instead of under 200 boys there has seemed to be twice that

number. Tramp, tramp, down the wooden gangway
they come.

"Can you picture the great hatch down below,
painted white, where long wooden tables and benches
accommodate the boys for meals? Come down with
me and see those rows and rows of figures, clad in
navy blue, with closely cropped heads. And there are
the stewards in white coats ready to serve."

Storms at sea made lasting impressions upon the children. One
Barnardo Girl remembered:

"A terrible storm came up. Mr. and Mrs. Hobday
gathered us children into the ship's mess hall. They
prayed committing us orphans to his care. Then I
shall never forget, I can hear it yet, as the wind whipped and rocked the ship, two hundred children's
voices singing from our small red Sankey Hymn Book:

'Eternal father strong to save;
Whose arm hath bound the restless wave,
Who bids't the mighty ocean deep
It's own appointed limits keep
Oh! hear us when we cry to Thee
For those in peril on the sea.' "

CANADA AHOY!

The Atlantic conquered, the great emigrant ship cut motors
as it neared the foggy shores of Newfoundland where mass ice
fields created dense fog. The children marvelled that such great
ice bergs, complete with polar bears, slipped past so silently. The
fog signal sounded at Belle Isle and the ship slipped into the blue
waters of the Gulf of St. Lawrence.

The last twenty-four hours of the voyage and the first forty-
eight after landing in Canada were the busiest. At two a.m., entering
the St. Lawrence River, the ship's stewards hauled hundreds of
Barnardo trunks on deck. Keys were handed out to Barnardo staff
members who proceeded to unlock each trunk. At five o'clock,
each child was marched on deck, assigned to his trunk where he
disrobed and changed into fresh clothing. He was ready to land in
Canada.

The selection of immigration ports varied depending upon the attitude of immigration authorities and the convenience of transportation. Barnardo children entered at Saint John, New Brunswick; Halifax, Nova Scotia; Portland, Maine; and Point Levis, Quebec. The most frequently used entrance to Canada was the St. Lawrence where the river pilot embarked at Point au Père, 150 miles below Quebec, to guide the ship inland towards the harbour. The St. Lawrence pilot brought for Barnardo's Canadian Superintendent, Mr. Owen, new applications from Canadian farmers seeking Barnardo Children as farm apprentices or domestics.

In accordance with the Canadian Immigration Department regulations, the children were cleared by the Chief Medical Inspector who checked for trachoma which involved the painful turning back of the eyelid. If the child was approved, his landing card was stamped. Once Mr. A.B. Owen signed the admission form, the child was officially admitted to the land of his adoption.

Admission Form

"I do solemnly declare that the 200 children named in the following are brought out to Canada for the purpose of settling therein, that they have not been inmates of workhouses, and that they have passed a satisfactory medical inspection at the point of departure; and I make this solemn declaration, conscientiously believing it to be true and knowing that it is of the same force and effect as if made under oath and by virtue of the Canada Evidence Act 1893.

Signed A. B. Owen

Declared before the Justice of the Peace.

BARNARDO SPECIAL

At Point Levis, hundreds of Barnardo children boarded the passenger cars of the special train provided by the Grand Trunk. They passed along the southern shore of Quebec, through Richmond and into the sheds at Montreal where refueling and fresh farm eggs were taken aboard to feed hundreds of children heading into Ontario. Past Belleville, where Annie MacPherson's Canadian Home was located, on through Cobourg, then to Port Hope and northward where the Grand Trunk jerked and squealed past farm steads to which some of the children would return. Dawn broke on freshly

*The Barnardo Special, Grand Trunk Line. Thousands of
Children pumped into Canada's life line*
— Courtesy The Hans McKee Collection

ploughed fields, sparkling rivers and vast woodlands. The children's
imaginations were startled for they had been forested in bricks and
concrete. Hundreds of children pulsed along Canada's iron artery
into Canada's heartland.

Tranpsorting hundreds of children inland required organization
and patience. In 1898, a Barnardo staff person in charge of the
Barnardo Children commented:

> "On the last night of our journey when our train
> compartment was strewn with slumbering figures
> along comes Mr. Owen to tell us that in half an hour
> our train will be divided so that one half will go
> direct to Toronto while the rest remain four hours
> at the Junction then to be taken on to Peterborough.

> "Lo! I am left with 150 odd girls (odd only in
> numbers) to continue alone on our way to Peter-
> borough. Relieved some hours later by a hasty wash
> all round in a borrowed bucket and breakfast served
> out of a tub, we counted and recounted our two
> carriages of girls to find all complete. Did I say
> complete? Well, there were caps missing, a shoe
> lost and some spectacles that could not be found,
> but that did not count; the girls were all there. At
> 8 a.m., with the train bell's clang! clang! we steamed
> up to the Peterborough platform there to deliver up
> our charge."

PART III

"Canada! thou art a noble, free, and rising
Country–the great fostering mother of the orphans
of civilization. . , thou must be great, and I will and
do love thee, land of my adoption."

Susanna Moodie,
Roughing It in the Bush

Rural Canada — Manitoba Archives

O CANADA

"No lion shall her fright,
she will with giants fight,
she hath a right
to be a pilgrim."

Pilgrim's Progress

BARNARDO GIRLS IN CANADA

On July 25th, 1883, seventy-two Barnardo Girls under the care of Barnardo's staff member, Miss Emilie Morecroft, prepared to sail for Canada. This was the first female emigration into Canada under Barnardo auspices. Mrs. Barnardo recalled the parting day:

> "His little girls had gathered round him on board
> the Sardinia, as he committed them to God, his
> heart would fain have let the tender leave without
> him. But he had earnest hopes of seeing them
> shortly, and towards the end of 1883 he publically
> declared his resolve to visit Canada next year."

When the shipload of Barnardo's female proteges landed at Quebec, news reached the party that George A. Cox, Mayor of Peterborough and President of the Midland Railway Company of Canada had offered rent-free a large house called Hazelbrae to receive the children. Doctor Barnardo wrote:

> "I cannot be too thankful to God for this goodness
> in touching the hearts of this gentleman and his wife,
> neither of whom I have ever seen, to offer such aid."

Earl Cairns, Lord Chancellor of Great Britain and President of the Barnardo Board, sent to Mayor George Cox and Mrs. Cox a letter of gratitude.

HAZELBRAE

George Albertus Cox, benefactor of the Barnardo emigration into Canada, was the ideal model for aspiring young emigrants. Orphaned at the age of five and nurtured in an agrarian environment where hard work and determination were considered virtues, he rose to become the centre of Canadian commerce.

From his birth place at Colborne, Ontario, he followed the iron artery into Peterborough, the "cultural oasis" of Canada's backwoods where he found enterprising people with faith in the land, in the people and in the iron rail. Here he cultivated friendships and business liasons with entrepreneurs among whom were James Wallis, the Haultains, (Sir) Sandford Fleming and (Sir) Joseph Flavelle. By 1872, George Cox was Mayor of Peterborough and shortly after that entered into provincial politics. By 1885, he was recognized in Canadian business circles as a "financial genius". His ventures into railway, real estate, insurance, banking and industry set up many of Ontario's major corporations. In 1898 he was appointed to the Canadian Senate.

In the spirit of all great men and women, George and Margaret Cox were sensitive to human misery and needs around them. They were key support figures in financing institutions that attempted to uplift the human spirit. Cox's interest in the Barnardo Children was triggered in 1883 while on business in Toronto when he was invited by members of Barnardo's Canadian Committee (among whom were his associates S.H. Blake, Q.C. and (Sir) William Mulock) to meet Alfred de Brissac Owen, Barnardo's energetic Canadian Superintendent and Frederick Fielder, the Governor of Barnardo's London headquarters. Cox accompanied the gentlemen to Peterborough where "Hazelbrae" was selected as the first Barnardo Home in Canada.

Hazelbrae was "an elegant brick mansion" three stories high, standing on five acres of land at the junction of the Cobourg-Peterborough line and the Grand Trunk rail line. The house dated as early as 1840 when Dominion land surveyor, Edward Caddy, resided there. The last private householders were Alex and Elizabeth Smith. In 1883, Mayor Cox secured the property and Hazelbrae was renovated from a private residence into a home capable of housing hundreds of children. The drawing room was converted into a well lighted play room and the large kitchen was lined with long wooden tables to feed hundreds of children. Mr. Cox had a large annex affixed to the building. This wing contained a lavatory on the ground floor and sleeping quarters for 150 children on the second and third levels. Each child had a small cot, "neatly made up," a grey blanket and a spotless pillow. The *Peterborough Examiner* reported: "To a lad or girl, whose memories go back a few months to the time when their softest couch was under a cart or archway, in a coal bus, or in the more sheltered but more repulsive lodging houses, these comfortable beds will be Abraham's bosom."

In 1884, the town bustled with committees preparing for the arrival of the children and their benefactor, Dr. Barnardo.

Mrs. Haultain, mother of Sir Frederick Haultain, snapped photos of Hazelbrae with her new Kodak and sold them as a fund raising project. Bazaar objects and articles of clothing stimulated sewing bees.

Katherine E. Wallis, sculptor, composed verse in celebration:

> "On charitable deeds intent
> Our Effie (Haultain) to her Uncles' went,
> To meet her friends, who there did sew
> To help good Doctor Barnardo."

Louisa Forbes Wallis, the "Jenny Lind" of Upper Canada and chatelaine of Merino wrote in her diary: "Dr. Barnardo is coming to Peterborough and I shall have him to Merino. He is doing a wonderful work for the good of humanity."

In a letter to the editor of the *Peterborough Examiner,* 1884, the Governor of Stepney Causeway wrote concerning the acquisition of Hazelbrae by Dr. Barnardo's.

> "Sir,
>
> It may be known to some of your readers that Mr. Geo. A. Cox has very kindly and generously given the commodious house, recently owned by Mrs. Alex Smith, known as "Hazelbrae", to be used as the Canadian Branch of Dr. Barnardo's Homes, London, England. Mr. and Mrs. Cox, General and Mrs. Haultain and others in the town, have for a considerable length of time, taken a warm and active

interest in the work which these institutions are doing. The house will be arranged as to accommodate at least 120 children, but so large a number would not remain, as the demand for these children has hitherto proved so great as to warrant the belief that it will not be necessary for the permanent maintenance of more than fifty. It ought to be observed, too, that the Home is not designed exclusively for children brought out from the parent institution. Destitute or orphan children in Peterborough itself will ever be eligible for admission, none such will ever be rejected, provided, of course, there is a vacancy."

BARNARDO STAFF

The original Barnardo staff was Canadian, consisting of Superintendents Mr. and Mrs. Edward Duff, Miss Millie Sanderson, Secretary, and Mr. A. B. Owen, travelling agent.

Miss Millie Sanderson, teacher, and Mr. and Mrs. Edward Duff, Superintendents of the Canadian Barnardo Home were sent to England to study the Barnardo method and bring back the first boat load of children under Canadian auspices.

Miss Sanderson stayed in the Girls' Garden Village where she prepared and selected girls to enter Canada.

In *Nights and Days* , 1883, Miss Sanderson recorded her talks with the young emigrants.

"I talked to them about my fair land across the sea, with its wooded hills and well-tilled plains, the beautiful streams and broad blue lakes, its mighty forests and its towering rocks, whose strange weird echoes, like woodland elves mimic the wild birds' cry. I told them of the gorgeous hues of the autumn leaves. . . and the soft white mantle that is spread over the earth by the winter sky. Then their eyes grew big with wonder as I described the curious bridge of ice built by clever Jack Frost over lakes and rivers changing the merry flow of their summer waves into the still whiteness that the red men say 'The waters have gone to sleep.'

"But this was all like a fairy tale; and as I did not think it fair to hide from them the darker tintings of

the emigrant picture. I told them of short summers
and weary winters, when all the poetry of life seems
to be either parched with heat or shrivelled with cold;
and then I spoke to them of work–not slavery– but
honest, intelligent labour, and gave them clearly to see
that drones have no more chance in a Canadian than
in an English hive. Good hard work, is the order of
the day, and commands good wages; and a girl who
is active and willing, honest and true is sure to find a
comfortable home and kindhearted friends. Her
chances of success lie within herself and will be mea-
sured by the brightness or stupidity with which she
manages those ten good servants her own young
fingers.

"Some of my girls pulled long faces while others
brightened up as if they thought of the difficulties to
be met and conquered only roused their girlish ambi-
tions. Such girls as these were sent out with knowledge of what lies before them, and their young
hearts stirred to be and do their best and they are
sure to do well."

In 1884, one hundred and thirty little girls "volunteered" for
Canada. Miss Sanderson recorded the departure in *Nights and Days*:

"Dear Mr. Editor: (Dr. Barnardo)

Were English skies tearfully regretful at our departure that 10th of July, that they poured out
such copious showers. . . ? It would indeed seem for
the sky wept continously. As we traversed from the
great metropolis under your own escort, I need not
recount the incidents nor since you accompanied the
party, is it necessary to remind you of the long pro-
cession of brown ulsters and red hoods that marched
cheerily through the pouring rain from Lime Street
station to Liverpool Docks, and then on board the
steamer. . .

"After seeing our one-hundred-and-twenty bairns
snugly stowed away in their berths, under the kindly
care of their stewardess, we all felt intensely weary;
but, above and beyond the need of physical rest, rose

Miss Bessie Code at Hazelbrae — Centennial Museum, Peterborough

Senator George Albertus Cox Mayor of Peterborough 1872-74; 1884-85

Alfred deBrissac Owen Barnardo's Canadian Superintendent 1883-1922

such a sense of responsibility and personal helplessness, that we knelt together and poured out our hearts before God. . .

"Towards the end of our voyage we were so befogged for a couple days, that we made but little progress; but by the good hand of God and the skill of our watchful captain, we were brought safely through, although immense fields of ice surrounded us, some of the largest bergs seeming perilously near. Under bright blue skies, and with favouring breezes, we entered the Gulf of St. Lawrence, and soon the children's eyes grew big with wonder as the good ship made its way into the beautiful waters of the river of the same name.

"Landing at Point Levis, just opposite Quebec,. . . we experienced Mr. Stafford's kindness in many ways. Here, too, we were speedily joined by Mr. Owen, by whose kindly forethought every accommodation possible under the circumstances had been secured for our comfort during our long railway journey from Quebec to Peterboro'. Supper had been prepared for our party at the Emigration Refreshment Rooms; and the exclamations of delight over 'two eggs apiece' must have been gratifying to those who had so kindly provided the treat.

"Another tiresome night over, we found ourselves at Belleville, and were told that in a few hours our wearisome journey would be ended. We had a very lively time during the last two hours, the excitement deepening as we drew near Peterboro'. To me it meant coming home, and therefore, the speed of the train seemed little better than a snail's pace.

On Monday, 21st the "Barnardo Special" pulled into Peterborough. Mayor George Cox and prominent citizens waited the arrival of the notable Doctor Barnardo and his little proteges. Applications had already been received for all the girls but they were retained at the house until after a public reception.

At 8 o'clock, carriages, hacks and vehicles of various descriptions rolled up George Street followed by the Fire Brigade Band accompanied by foot passengers on either side. The main drive up to Hazelbrae was illumined by Chinese lanterns hung from trees.

The lawns were spotted with chairs and tables of lemonade.

Inside tables filled with food were spread for the children in the school room. Refreshments and bazaar items were sold. Over 700 people filed through Hazelbrae, 10 cents admission being charged. At nine o'clock the 130 children were placed row upon row on the spacious staircase where they sang several songs. Golden opinions were expressed of the musical training received in the British Homes. Gifts from the bazaar tables were given to the children who were packed off to bed in readiness for their journeys to the country.

While the children spent their first night in Canada, Dr. Barnardo was ushered to the newly opened Bradburn Opera House and the *Peterborough Examiner* reported the momentous occasion.

In 1889, George A. Cox and his wife Margaret moved to Toronto as had fellow Peterburian and millionaire Joseph Flavelle. The work at Hazelbrae suffered. Dr. Barnardo wrote: "During the continued residence of Mr. and Mrs. Cox at Peterborough, their personal interest in the Institution did much to promote its success; but of late years, to my great regret and to real loss of the work, Mr. and Mrs. Cox have removed their home to Toronto."

In 1890, Thomas Barnardo sailed once more for Canada. He wrote:

>"The growth of our work led to such changes in organization that I found it necessary to pay personal visits to the Institutions which had been formed under my auspices in Canada. I left England by the Polynesian, Allan Line. I did not linger long at Quebec, and remained only two days at Montreal, before proceeding to our Institution at Peterborough. I reached Peterborough late in the afternoon of a lovely and unexpectedly cool and pleasant day in midsummer. A warm greeting awaited me. The children, resident in the house, and the ladies resident of the staff, were all assembled on the veranda .

>"Recent changes had occurred since my visit of 1887. Captain and Mrs. Annesley and their daughter, Miss Annesley with an old servant of theirs who had filled the post of Kitchen Matron,

The Peterborough Examiner

Thursday, August 21, 1884

AN HOUR WITH DR. BARNARDO

Graphic Sketch of Dr. Barnardo's Great Work–His Description of the Waifs and Strays of London. The Way the Work is Wrought, its Success and Extent–Hazel Brae Branch Peterborough, Generosity.

On Thursday evening last, Dr. T.J. Barnardo, the great practical London philanthropist, delivered a discourse of thrilling interest on the subject of the "Waifs and Strays" of the World's Metropolis London.

At the hour for beginning, every seat in the capacious Bradburn Opera House was occupied, both floor and galleries, and supplementary seats had to be furnished. John Burnham, Esq. M.P. for East Peterborough, occupied the chair and there were on the platform, besides the following, reverend gentlemen–Rev. Mr. Davis, Rev. Mr. Brown, St. John's, Rev. Mr. Bell, St. Andrew's, Rev. Mr. McAmmond, Ashburnham, Methodist, Geo. A. Cox, and Mr. Edward Duff, Superintendent of Hazel Brae.

The hymn, "Rescue the Perishing," was sung, and Rev. Mr. Brown offered prayers.

The chairman, John Burnham, M.P., said he had much pleasure in being present on the occasion, and the large audience present was a proof of the great interest the people of Peterborough felt in the work carried on by Dr. Barnardo who was well known to all by reputation in fact his name was a household word. He highly commended the noble work in which he was engaged. Citizens of Canada could not, from the absence of want and misery here, appreciate the great work carried on among the teeming millions of London. He said he had learned from the report that eighteen years ago, Dr. Barnardo had become interested in one homeless boy, and from that interest had sprung many well-organized and well-equipped homes, giving shelter and instruction to about 1,300 otherwise homeless orphans. The revenue for the support of these homes had increased from $1,000 a year to $225,000. He dealt with the objection of some persons to the introduction of children into Canada. The feeling was not general, for there was room in the broad Dominion for every soul likely to become a good and industrious citizen.

The sympathy of Peterborough was more directly aroused, owing to the beneficence and bounty of Mr. and Mrs. Geo. A. Cox by whose liberality a branch of the homes had been set up here.

But said John Burnham the work appealed to more than their sympathy, it demanded their contributions, which he had no doubt would be given willingly.

Dr. Barnardo, who on coming forward was received with warm applause and that in dealing with his subject he was not at loss to make his audience understand the conditions upon which the work was founded.

had retired from the work, as also had Miss Sanderson, the first resident Secretary."

Hazelbrae was not the *coleur de rose,* although, Miss Woodgate, the new Matron had the servants and children respectful and quiet. But Barnardo's greatest concern was that his female proteges had already encountered "a great deal of the seamy side of Canadian life and that sending young girls into isolated rural farms brought new concern to the Institutions."

Barnardo recorded his concern:

"I can never tell under what great public crisis here I may suddenly be compelled to supply information, and even to reporduce the reports themselves which give the most ample proof of minute, motherly, womanly care of such defenceless creatures, placed under conditions which are not natural to them, but which I have created as an exercise of my own will. My heart cries out within me nor can any words which I can utter express my feeling."

In 1889 Miss Margaret Stent, Honourary Secretary of the Girls' Village, Ilford was sent to Canada to report on the emigration system as affecting the girls and to carry out urgently needed reform. As a result of Miss Stent's research Doctor Barnardo stated that no girls would be handed over to any mistress who did not give formal pledge that she would never be absent from the house one night without taking care that the young girl committed to her was left in the custody of some respectable woman, and that no girl shall be allowed to work under conditions which place her in circumstances of unrestrained intimacy with persons of the opposite sex, without adequate supervision from her mistress.

In 1889 Hazelbrae became sole headquarters for girls. The receiving, distribution and oversight of the boys was transferred from Peterborough to 214 Farley Ave., Toronto. By 1912 Dr. Barnardo's Home, Peterborough was renamed the "Margaret Cox Home for Girls", in honour of Mrs. George A. Cox, who had taken such an interest in providing a Canadian Home for children.

In 1918, George A. Cox's son, Herbert Cox, willed the Hazelbrae property to Doctor Barnardo's Institute. Four years later, child emigration into Canada was slowing down. The Hazelbrae Home was closed and Barnardo's Canadian headquarters for both boys and girls, was moved to 538 Jarvis Street, the stately home of Cawthra Mulock, the deceased son of William Mulock, Ontario's Chief Justice. In 1939, Hazelbrae, Peterborough, Dr. Barnardo's first Home for children in Canada, was torn down, the only memorial to its existence, Barnardo Street. The *Peterborough Examiner* reported:

Barnardo Home Is Being Razed

"Perhaps, some day these timbers will be used in homes, not so fine and large, but they will again ring to the joys and tears of human life. Mothers and grandmothers now look back upon the old mansion as their first pleasant memory of this country. In May, 1922, after serving for 39 years as a home for Barnardo Girls, the house was closed forever."

Marchmont Home, Belleville
Amalgamated with Dr. Barnardo's Homes, Toronto

Rev. and Mrs. Robert Wallace
Superintendents

Miss Annie MacPherson
Dr. Barnardo's Associate

Barnardo's of London purchased Marchmont in 1925. Some of the Hazelbrae staff were transferred to Belleville
— Barnardo Archives

CHRISTMAS DAY

1896

Children had a merry day of it indeed. On their
return from attending service in the George Street
church in the morning, the entire staff dined with
them in the large dining hall, where huge portions
of turkey and English plum pudding served to make
the little ones think they were back in Old England
again or rather made them glad they were not, as what
the majority of them knew of such good things in the
mother country was gathered by the tales told by more
fortunate children who, at least, had a home to boast
of. However under the guarding wings of the good
angel who guided these little waifs into Dr. Barnardo's
care, it is hoped that for them all will be plain sailing
hereafter and the day for them is past when a Christmas
dinner is only a myth and not such a substantial reality
as it was yesterday at the Home.

At the conclusion fo their hearty meal the children
were taken to the schoolroom which was elaborately
decorated with evergreens, and in the corner of which
stood a gigantic Christmas tree. Mr. Metcalfe, in fur
coat and great hoary white whiskers, enacted the part
of old Father Christmas, and distributed the gifts to
the thoroughly delighted little ones. At the conclusion
of this part of the programme the room was cleared
of furniture and the children were allowed to indulge
in those round games which are so dear to the heart
of every child. In the evening bonbons and sweets
were distributed and the games were continued until
bedtime, closing a day which was probably fraught with
more pleasure for the children than any of them had
ever experienced in the past.

Evening Examiner

FROM SEA TO SEA

1912

There is not to-day an accessible part of the Dominion of Canada, where Barnardo boys and girls are not be found, from Nova Scotia to the Yukon; from Lake Erie to the Mackenzie River. If at Christmas we could uncover the roofs of a few thousand Canadian dwellings, we should witness scenes that would assuredly gladden the hearts of all who wish well and think well of our work. We should see many of our old boys and girls, now fathers and mothers of families, gathering their own boys and girls around them in homes that, in many cases, are replete with every comfort. There would be many hundreds of little boarded-out youngsters eager to see what Santa Claus had put in their stockings. We should witness family gatherings at which the Home boy or girl is made as welcome as the sons and daughters of the household.

The sketch might be extended almost indefinitely. For we have at the end of the year under review a record of 24,041 emigrants set to Canada to draw upon. Some of these went out by one and twos, as far back as 1870. Nine hundred and thirteen of them went in 1912. If ever a movement was justified by its fruits, it is our Canadian Emigration. By emigration we may well be content to stand or fall, and our enemies themselves (if we have any) may be the judges. But indeed, our young people in Canada, by the successes they have won and the respect they have inspired, have stopped the mouths of lions." The enemies of thirty years ago have been converted into very mild critics, if not even enthusiastic friends. And now to-day we find 95 per cent, of those who are still alive on the high road to prosperity. Many of them have arrived at a pitch and goal of prosperity which once upon a time would have seemed to them as unattainable as the crown of England.

Ups and Downs

Dr. Barnardo's Canadian Headquarters, 1922; 532 Jarvis Street, Toronto, Ontario   — Barnardo Archives

Lady Superintendent Rose Hobday and Barnardo Girls
— Public Archives, Ottawa

APPLICATION FOR A BARNARDO CHILD

Canadians wishing to secure the services of a Barnardo Boy or Girl made application to the Home. The agreement was drawn up in simple language, free from legal verbiage between the applicant and Barnardo's of Canada. It stated that the child, until age 18 (boys) or 21 (girls), was under the guardianship of the Homes. The employer agreed to receive the child for a period beginning and ending on specified dates and was to provide the child with sufficient and proper board.

Between the ages of 8 and 13, the child was "placed-out", receiving room and board in exchange for farm labour which Barnardo hoped would be "no more and no less than the farmer's own children." Barnardo stated, "To overwork and make a drudge of little boys or girls of ten or eleven would be a wrong to be condemned."

At 14 the child was expected to negotiate with the employer for monthly wages in exchange for his labour.

LEAVING FOR A SITUATION

Once the Barnardo contract had been signed the child prepared to leave for his situation. He was provided with: a lunch, a railway ticket, a destination card, his Barnardo trunk, a letter of introduction, an envelope containing two addressed postcards and a little booklet entitled "Directions on Leaving for Situations" which recorded the child's responsibilities to his employer and the employer's towards the child.

The editor of the *Ups and Downs* commented, "Of course the boys are considerably more interested in their lunch packages than in their little books and assimilate the contents of one much more speedily than the other."

RURAL PLACEMENTS

From Toronto and Peterborough hundreds of children were pumped through Canada's iron artery into rural placements where these child pioneers encountered the ups and downs of a pre-industrialized agrarian society.

Despite the Spartan-like existence on the average Canadian farm Barnardo believed that his proteges would be better off in rural Canada than in over-crowded cities in England where they would be trapped in the poverty cycle. In Great Britain's over-populated cities a child was "a rope around one's neck", while in rural Canada children were considered to be a source of great wealth. Case studies reveal that without the assistance of children, as farm labourers and domestics, progress on the Canadian farm was almost impossible. Barnardo argued that the education his proteges received on the Canadian farm equipped them for future usefulness and success in Canadian life.

Life on the Canadian farm was challenging. From being cared for in Barnardo's British Homes, equipped with clothing and training, the children encountered Canada's wilderness, where houses were scattered miles and miles apart and where animals, weather and people were all foreign to their urban background.

Extremes encountered by the Barnardo Child on the Canadian farm were recorded by British journalists. W. J. Bready, author of Doctor Barnardo, portrayed the Barnardo Child "free to roam the fields, explore the woods, pick wildflowers, chase rabbits, chipmunks and squirrels, while in the winter, he was free to skate, snow-shoe, sled, toboggan and snowball to his heart's content." On the other hand, British newspapers, hostile to the emigration, saw the emigrant child as being forced to labour in sub-zero weather, eating dry crusts and water while being slowly murdered by a fiendish Canadian farmer and his wife, who as soon as they had used up one Barnardo Child, applied for another.

Mr. A. B. Owen, Barnardo's Canadian Superintendent suggested:

> "Compare the lot of the ordinary Barnardo boy
> on an ordinary Canadian farm, and under an ordinary
> Canadian farmer, with the lot of boys elsewhere—of
> boys who are working in factories and shops, of boys
> at sea, apprentices, errand boys or bell-boys. We do
> not hestitate to say that on the average the farm boy
> has far more of the sweets and far less of the hard
> and bitter things in life than all but a very few of his
> contemporaries. His surroundings are healthier, his
> relations with his employer are more friendly and
> sympathetic, his work has infinitely more interest
> and variety, his food is superior, he is better housed,
> his general comforts are better cared for than those
> of the same class, and he experiences far less of any-
> thing like real privations or hardship."

In 1908, Barnardo calculated that 90% of his importations were still in agrarian settlements, "attached to the land, making two potatoes grow where one grew before, and contributing in this way to the wealth of the country."

BANK ACCOUNTS

Each Barnardo Child in Canada was issued an account with the Bank of Commerce of which George A. Cox was President. In 1912, the Manager of the Bank of Commerce stated that the wages due the boys and girls were remitted direct to the bank where individual accounts were opened in the name of the General Superintendent. The pass book was sent to the child or back to the Home. No withdrawal could be made without permission of the Barnardo Home. When the child was 18(boys) or 21 (girls), no longer wards of Barnardo's, the monies could be withdrawn.

Barnardo was proud of the earning power of his proteges. *Ups and Downs* noted

> "that the stock of the Bank of Commerce has
> lately risen several points on the money market. We
> do not flatter ourselves that this is attributable to the
> business of the Barnardo Homes, but we can claim that
> the Bank of Commerce is only one of the many Can-
> adian institutions that directly or indirectly profits
> from the thrift, industry and increasingly valuable
> earning power of the Dr. Barnardo's young colonists."

VISITATION

Barnardo attempted to maintain contact with his proteges through visitation and correspondence. Of his system of inspection he stated: "Surprise visits are paid to my young people all over the Dominion by Gentlemen and Lady Visitors." The visiting personnel were to remove the child if abuse or dissatisfaction were apparent. Rewards for endurance were given to those who remained on Canadian farms for extended periods. Barnardo, himself, stated that every time the child removed from his placement he "dragged a lengthening chain."

Although Barnardo promised systematic visitation many children in isolated areas never saw a Barnardo visitor. The immense distance, the challenging Canadian roads and weather led to Visitors' confessions:

"I was not able to get to W___ to see Colin H.,
the roads being quite washed away by floods. I
went on in hopes of visiting Harry C. and his sister
Mary who is in service about five miles from him,
but here was the same story, positive waterfalls where
the roads should be. Myself and Mr. B. have been
travelling five days, soaked to the skin every day and
all to no purpose. I will not now be able to get to
these young people until next year, when it is to be
hoped the Lord will abate the tempest."

The second method of attempting to keep in touch with
Barnardo proteges was through the Canadian publication *Ups and
Downs*. In 1890 the *Globe and Mail* announced:

"The Canadian Manager of the Barnardo Homes,
Mr. A. B. Owen, has decided to publish a monthly
journal which is hoped will not only maintain the
interest in and oversight of the Barnardo Children
who have come to Canada under the auspices of Dr.
Barnardo, but also for the children themselves."

Ups and Downs was published quarterly; the format of the magazine
included editorials, letters, and photos. Letters from the Barnardo
Children were published along with their photos. All material was
highly editorialized and unfortunate experiences, sadness or loneliness deleted. Barnardo Children subscribed to the magazine
through their earnings. It provided, in many cases, a sense of belonging to the "largest family in the world." After W.W.I the
publication closed its Canadian offices and the *Guild Messenger,*
London, contained Canadian news.

ADOPTION OF BARNARDO CHILDREN

Barnardo's Infant Colony

By the turn of the century, Barnardo felt it was necessary to
establish an infant colony in Canada. The expanded British facility
which housed homeless infants was filled.

The Canadian infant colony was located in a rural and healthy
part of Ontario, not far from one of the great towns where medical
staff and facilities were convenient.

The first summer, the infants were affected by serious intestinal complaints and several lost their lives, while the rest were weakened. The severe Canadian winter caused the infants to succumb to respiratory diseases and the death-rate increased at an alarming rate. The mortality rate, during the seventeen months in which this Canadian infant colony experiment was conducted, rose to 20% per annum, a death rate of 200 per 1000. Alarmed and fearful of adverse publicity Barnardo consulted with medical authorities in Canada and decided not to emigrate infant children.

Once the colony was closed Barnardo's mortality rate dropped to 4% per thousand per annum and even in years when several accidents claimed the lives of Barnardo Boys and Girls, the death rate never exceeded 8% per thousand per annum.

If Doctor Barnardo's infant colony in Canada had been successful very young children could have been secured by childless couples and absorbed at an early age into the Canadian landscape. When the colony collapsed, Barnardo's youngest children were five or six. These children were eligible for adoption. In Barnardo's first shipload of children there were "fifty bright little girls, who as call may be made on them will be drafted off to Christian households for adoption."

In the early 1800's the term "adoption" in both England and Canada meant to take a child under an employment contract. In 1874, Andrew Doyle's report defined adoption through the eyes of a homeless child who said, "adoption, sir, is when folks get a girl to work without wages."

By 1884, when emigration was in full swing, Barnardo's realized the dangers in adoption. The Canadian Superintendent stated:

> "There was always the risk of adoption being simply
> a plausible excuse for employing the services of a child
> without paying for them until the boy or girl realized
> that they were being impossessed upon."

Although exceptions to "boarding-out" were made in case of children between five and nine, Barnardo noted a curiously large demand for little ones to be adopted in childless families comparatively wealthy.

"One boy," commented Barnardo, "whom I rescued from very degraded and even dangerous surroundings, looked like the son of a gentleman, when years afterwards, I met him in Canada. He had been sent to University, was well educated, and thoroughly refined in manner and I could not help avoid mentally contrasting his present with his past."

MALTREATMENT

". . . and some fell on rough ground."

Luke 8

Burial Cairn, Russell, Manitoba

The placement of thousands of dependent children in rural situations scattered across the Dominion was an awesome task and Barnardo admitted that despite careful screening there were employers "who are far from desirable guardians or associates of young children."

Reports, written and oral, indicate that many Barnardo children were subjected to various forms of maltreatment: sexual assault, beatings, accidents with pitchforks, impalements on fenceposts. Gross forms of human indecency and inhumanity were inflicted on some of these dependent children and youth.

Immobilized by fear and cloistered in isolation many of the children were subjected to emotional and psychological abuse stemming from an immature and prejudiced mentality. In some school areas, board members ran on an anti-Barnardo platform. Hostile attitudes wishing that the ships that brought the children would sink mid-Atlantic; condemnation of the children as "tainted gutter-snips" polluting Canada's "virgin soil" were voiced by a vocal minority.

BARNARDO HOME PLOT

A selection from the REGISTER OF INTERNMENTS at
Little Lake Cemetary, Peterborough, Ontario

NAME	RELATIVES	AGE	PLACE OF BIRTH	PLACE OF DEATH AND DATE	CAUSE OF DEATH
George Beagle	Barnardo Home	17	England	Otonabee River, 1885	accidentally drowned
Harriet Beeley	Barnardo Home	16	England	Peterborough, 1888	brain disease
Elizabeth Birch	Barnardo Home	12	England	Peterborough, 1889	accidently drowned
Ellen Robinson	Barnardo Home	9	England	Peterborough, 1895	scarlet fever & paralysis
Louisia Boyle	Barnardo Home	17	England	Peterborough, 1894	typhoid fever
Esther Rondeau	Barnardo Home	23	England	Peterborough, 1895	consumption
Ada Barker	Barnardo Home	18	England	Hastings, 1896	pneumonia
Bertha Pickering	Barnardo Home	14	England	Peterborough, 1896	consumption
Jane Buddle	Barnardo Home	10	England	Peterborough, 1898	phthipis
Jane Loveday	(Secretary)	55	England	Ottawa, 1906	burned in Gilmour House Fire
Ivy Plant	Barnardo Home	16	England	Peterborough, 1913	asthemia
Alfred Punicard	Barnardo Home	14	England	Peterborough, 1914	cerebral spinal meningitis
Adelaide Pearce	(Teacher)	45	England	York, 1918	Phthipis Pulmonotis
Isabella Bidwell	Barnardo Home	23	England	Peterborough, 1920	influenza pneumonia

The term "Home Child" was coined carrying with it the connotation of second-class citizenship. In 1911 Barnardo's Canadian Superintendent stated that "some Canadians are prejudiced enough to imagine that taking a "Home child" into their households they are incurring the risks of having their throats cut in the night or waking to find their barns in flame."

Distress in some Barnardo Children led to suicide: drownings, hangings, and poisonings. Others learned to cope in various ways. Runaways were common. Yet Barnardo's admonished children for running away stating that this was a mark against their record. Unaccustomed to the immense distances and severe Canadian winters, children were found miles from their placements frost bitten or dead. The most successful runaway was Wallace Ford, film star, who ran out of Canada and into Hollywood fame.

Taken from an industrialized metropolis and placed in an isolated pre-industrial environment without kith or kin some children suffered severely enough to lead to illness and death. Sick children were returned to the Homes at Peterborough, Toronto, Russell, and Winnipeg. Memorials and common burial plots were located at Peterborough, Ontario and Russell, Manitoba.

Ups and Downs, 1903, reported the illness and subsequent death of a Barnardo Girl.

> "Last month we reported how well Rachel Hall
> became after some treatment for rheumatism. She
> left Hazelbrae apparently full of health and spirit
> to return to her Ingersoll home, and you may
> imagine how shocked we were to receive, on May
> 7th, a brief telegram to say she was dead. We are
> well assured that everything that mortals could do
> was done to save Rachel's Life."

NATION AND EMPIRE BUILDERS

In spite of the ups and downs encountered by thousands of these child pioneers, they continued to brave Canada's vast spaces and build a nation.

In 1893, Canada's High Commissioner to London, Sir Charles Tupper stated, "I am proud to stand here tonight to bear testimony to the great and good work which Dr. Barnardo's Homes are performing in that country. Among those that bear testimony is the Hon. John Carling, Minister of Agriculture and Immigration in Canada. After having subjected this great work to the most careful examination, he has placed on record that 98% of Barnardo Children in Canada have been successes."

In 1910 Lord Mount Stephen, the man whose financial skill and resource propelled the Canadain Pacific Railway across the continent, donated $300,000 in aid of emigrating Barnardo Children into Canada. The annual income from the invested sum totalled $15,000 which assisted 300 Barnardo Children into Canada each year. Lord Strathcona, a director of the C.P.R. and the man to drive the last spike followed Lord Stephen's example with a large donation, as did other prominent nation builders.

Barnardo's commented on the donations stating that these Canadians of enterprise, courage and financial skill would not have contributed money to any organization that they were not assured of benefiting Canada.

Sir Edward Clarke, P. C. speaking on behalf of the Barnardo Children in Canada stated: "I am devoted to Canada. I am rather fanatic in my views as to what Canada is to become. In my mind the twentieth century is to be Canada's century. It is because I am looking forward to the future of Canada and to the prosperity of that great Dominion, that there is, to my thinking, a national side as well as an individual side to the Homes, that as we are helping children, we are also forwarding the progress of the Empire."

The War Years

In 1914, despite the threat of war, shiploads of children continued to pour into Canada. The official Barnardo "war party" consisted of 175 children who arrived in September, 1914 aboard the Corinthian. Docking at Quebec, the children were greeted by the first Canadian contingent of Barnardo Boys to be stationed at

ROOT SEARCH

Frank to Canada

Winnifred to Canada

*George (Watts Naval School)
to South Africa*

*Mrs. Brown, Widow,
England*

*Joe (Watts Naval School)
to Australia*

*Admitted by their widowed mother to Dr. Barnardo's, the
Brown children emigrated to different parts of the world.
Over half a century of dedicated research passed before the
Browns were reunited.*

Salisbury Plains. Among those enlisted were third and fourth generation "six-footers" whom Barnardo's boasted had "hardihood of body and hardiness of resource" resulting from life on the Canadian farm.

Letters from Barnardo Boys at war poured into the Canadian office, Toronto.

Salisbury Plain 1914

Dear Mr. Owen,

I suppose that you will be surprised to know that I am with the soldiers sent with the first Canadian contingent. I am well and have been since leaving the land of the Maple Leaf. We had a fine trip across. The people gave us a hearty welcome and even kissed some of the boys.

It has rained every day here. We tramp through mud over the shoe tops.

Well, Mr. Owen I have been to see my mother and older brother that I left when I went to Canada six years ago and they were glad to see me back on the errand that I came.

I remain yours truly a Barnardo Boy,

Thomas Kirk,
Canadian Contingent.

Barnardo Girls, although encouraged to stay in Canada, also responded to the war cry. Hazelbrae staff noted that "several of our most patriotic spirits have been fired with zeal to go to the front where we hear their services have been indispensible."

Ups and Downs kept its readership informed with editorials, photos and letters from the field. Honour rolls were published and acts of heroism proudly heralded. Sir Max Aitken, M.P. gave the official story of one Barnardo Boy, Sergeant Hickey, who had risked his life in the interest of fellow soldiers. He was awarded the Victoria Cross, the rarest of all British presentations.

Eleven thousand Barnardo proteges enrolled in the Great War and over half of these were from Canada. Enlisting was one way to attempt to renew acquaintances with family. Several soldiers contacted Barnardo's, London hoping to secure information to assist in tracking down kin folk. Some family ties were re-established.

Yet those emigrated in childhood seldom wished to remain in England, a better life having been secured in Canada.

Between 1916 and 1919 emigration into Canada ceased. Then on May 21st, burdened with war orphans, Barnardo's sent out its first post-war party.

Up to the outbreak of the war approximately 1,000 Barnardo children had been emigrated each year into Canada. In 1924 a British Overseas Delegation visited Canada to inspect the work of child emigration societies. The report was not in favour of emigration of children to Canada based on the helplessness of the child and the possibility of overwork. The only condition on which the delegation would support child emigration into Canada was on the basis that the child was taken into the home as a member of the family and legally adopted. "In our opinion," Miss Bondfield, Chair person of the Delegation stated, "it is only in such circumstances that children of tender age and unaccompanied by their parents should be allowed to go into Canada."

In 1921 the Canadian Adolescent Act raised the school leaving age to sixteen and by 1925 children under this age were not emigrated. The last Barnardo emigration into Canada arrived July 8th, 1939. At this date, it was estimated that at least three out of every two hundred Canadians were Barnardo Boys or Girls and their descendants.

In 1939, Mr. and Mrs. John Hobday, Superintendents at 536 Jarvis Street, Barnardo's Canadian headquarters, retired to England. Mr. George Black set up an after-care station at 466 Briar Hill Avenue, Toronto. In 1963 the Canadian office was closed. All records were sent back to Barnardo's, London.

PART IV

"The eyes of the country were focused on the new Canada beyond the Precambrian wilderness of the Shield. Tupper was preparing for an autumn visit through which the railway would run. So was the Governor-General, Lord Lorne, with a covey of foreign newspaper men. The great North West boom was about to begin."

Pierre Burton, *The Last Spike*

WH CHAPMAN

BARNARDO CHILDREN

GO WEST

As the great railway schemes unfolded, the Canadian West experienced immense expansion. Large areas of magnificently fertile land opened for settlement and the demand for immigrants seemed insatiable. Dr. Barnardo visualized the bread basket of the world filled by the diligent labours of trained Barnardo youth.

Challenged by the possibilities of pioneering in Canada's North West Barnardo reported:

> "We will have to build our own houses, to break
> up the soil, to plow and sow, to stock and develop. .
> Should this scheme prosper, I will be able to place out
> upon the land not less than 200 big fellows every year."

In 1884 Dr. Barnardo travelled to Winnipeg and purchased sight unseen several acres of land near Russell, Manitoba for the Industrial Farm. He was then authorized by the Barnardo Board, London (of which Queen Victoria's son-in-law, Canada's Governor-General Lorne was to become Board President in 1889) and his Canadian Committee (which included his lawyer William Mulock, later Ontario's Chief Justice) to request a grant of land from the Canadian government.

Barnardo wrote to Charles Tupper, Canada's High Commissioner:

"My Committee, some of whom have consider-
able Canadian experience, would not be prepared to
accept any land which might be allotted to them by
the Government. As the chief support of the Manitoba
branch. . .will be derived, it is hoped, from the cultiva-
tion of the land which would be granted, it would be
of greatest importance to us that such land should be
of first rate quality and situated in the most favour-
able position.

"Should the Dominion Government not feel free
to co-operate with us to the extent or in the manner
we desire, or to such an extent as would make it
advisable for us to attempt an enterprise of that
character, I am instructed to make my way to the
United States and there endeavour to obtain land
in such positions as may best meet the requirements
of our growing institutions."

After two years of negotiating, Dr. Barnardo secured land in
Canada's newly opened Northwest, near Russell, Manitoba. The area
contained rich loam deposits, rolling pasturage and a branch of the
Assineboine. By 1887, the Farm had acquired 8,900 acres.

Grants from the Manitoba and North-West Railway.	2,400 acres
Grants from the Manitoba Government. . . .	960
By purchase from the Manitoba and North-West Railway	960
Purchase of School Lands	640
Purchase from settlers and other parties . . .	4,000
Total	8,960 acres

Architects were assigned to design the Barnardo Industrial
Farm at a cost of L3,500.

"It is built of wood, and although I regret to
say to grave neglect, on the part of the Architects who had charge of its erection, it is anything but an ideal establishment, yet it has,
through the unceasing labours of the resident

manager, been made a fairly comfortable struc-
ture. On the ground floor is a large dining hall,
while dormitories occupy an equal space above.
There is a large entrance hall, and from the wind-
ows of the hospital-rooms on the second floor
is a view as charming as any that can be seen in
the North West."

Nights and Days 1887

Farm buildings consisting of large cow and horse stables, a piggery, a creamery, a pump house were stationed a distance from the main building.

As Manager of his Canadian Western Division, Thomas Barnardo attracted one of Manitoba's leading citizens, Edmund A. Struthers, formerly an inspector for the C.P.R. land department and railway immigration bureau to take charge of the Barnardo Children in Canada's West. Of Mr. Struthers and the Barnardo staff at the Industrial Farm, Russell, Barnardo recorded:

"Mr. Struthers, who has had a vast experience in
the North-West for many years, and who has occupied a position of responsibility and trust in connection with the Canadian Pacific Railway, is, as I
have already said, the chief head and responsible
Superintendent of our whole Institution. Mrs.
Struthers * ably seconds his efforts, and they are
supported by a Resident Master, who acts also as a
clerk, and his wife, who is the Matron Housekeeper,
together with such out-door assistance as so large
a farm, with its varied operations, and the supervision and instruction of so many lads, renders
necessary."

* Mary Vaughan Struthers

In 1887, Mr. Struthers went to Dr. Barnardo's Labour House, London and selected 34 youths for the Barnardo colonization programme. The cost to outfit and transport each youth from London to the Industrial Farm was Ł11 which under an agreement recognized by the Canadian government, stated that the emigrant was bound to give labour on the farm in return for his emigration costs.

Barnardo Youth selected for the Industrial Farm at Russell were from the London Labour House which boarded and trained unemployed youths between the ages of 17 and 20, with the understanding that at the end of an eight month apprenticeship, they would be emigrated to frontier life.

In 1887 Barnardo visited the Industrial Farm at Russell. The Barnardo Youth were marshalled on the open prairie for their benefactor's inspection who listened to Mr. Struthers' judgement of each and added a few words of encouragement, praise or "in a very few cases, admonition."

Nothing impressed Dr. Barnardo more than the great kindness the boys showed toward the stock.

> "In fact, I have never seen on a large farm, the same docility on the part of the dumb animals as I saw at Russell; a proof, if proof were wanting, of the great kindness of the boys. Many of these lads have, in their early lives, lacked love and kindly care; but now, with human hearts that yearn for something to love, they have lavished their sympathy upon the first living creature that was able, even in a dumb fashion, to appreciate and return kindly care."

The youth were trained at the Industrial Farm in all areas of agriculture in order to equip them for homesteading. There was keen competition among them in the matter of saving for their homestead. Barnardo noted that, "Some of their garments exhibited the most striking ingenuity. . . I never saw such picturesque patches in my life!" One looked less at their garments, than at the ruddy faces and bright eyes of vigourous homesteaders.

In 1889 Governor-General and Lady Stanley inspected Dr. Barnardo's Home at Russell, Manitoba. The *Dominion Illustrated* reported the arrival of the party.

> "On reaching the place, the inmates, sixty-four in number, were paraded in double lines, a bugle giving warning of the approach of the vice-regal party. The chief officials of the Institution, Mr. and Mrs. Struthers and the Rev. Mr. Drummond met His Excellency on the veranda of the Home and Mr. Kemp read an address in which the work of the Home was illustrated by the example of those who had prospered after leaving it. His

Edmund A. Struthers, Manager of Dr. Barnardo's Industrial Farm, (inset), Russell Manitoba and Barnardo Youth prepare for the arrival of Viscount Stanley, 1889.
— The Struthers Collection and the Manitoba Archives

Barnardo Youth ready to leave for Dr. Barnardo's Industrial Farm, Manitoba, 1888   *— Barnardo Archives*

Excellency replied in appropriate terms, dwelling upon
the advantages which the fine healthy looking lads before him enjoyed in this great, free, fertile country. . . "

Led by Mr. Struthers, the Governor-General toured the Farm, visiting
the boys' dormitory with its eighty neatly arranged beds, up to the
sick loft in the attic, then down to the dining room, the store and
workshop where they concluded their visitation with an inspection
of the farm buildings, livestock and creamery.

Reminding the Barnardo youth of the gratitude they owed
their benefactor, Lord Stanley praised Barnardo's homesteading
programme.

BARNARDO'S COLONIZATION SCHEME

"I am very hopeful that through God's goodness
by this means, a bright future is before the big rough
lads of our great cities, which may turn myriads of
lives into useful careers."

Barnardo, *Nights and Days*, 1887

The most important feature of Barnardo's emigration programme into the west, was that a young fellow who had shown steady
industry and honesty in course of a period of long service, would
be assisted by capital and otherwise to receive allotments of 160
acres each which the Canadian government offered to immigrants
over eighteen years of age. It was hoped that this plan would encourage good conduct on the part of the youths and make the farm
a colonizing centre for a large district in the vicinity.

With this in mind, Barnardo's colonization scheme was carried
out in accordance with the provisions of the Dominion Lands Act,
subject to the authority of the Minister of the Interior. Each year,
the Manager of the Farm secured from the Government a number of
quarter sections (160 acres) "with a view to giving the settlers
the advantages of good soil, wood and water, and reasonable prox-
imity to a railway." A habitable house and small stable were erected
on each quarter and the cost of the buildings formed part of the
advance made to the settler. Each Barnardo Boy assisted to a homestead had to give one hundred and fifty dollars to Mr. Struthers
and be eighteen years old. As soon as the location of the homestead had been determined and the entry made at the Land Office,
E. A. Struthers outfitted the Barnardo settler with an oxen, plough,

cart, harness and provisions to start his homestead. Additional materials including implements, stock, seed, building materials and labour were charged to the settler at lowest cost. The settler could also borrow machinery from the Farm at lowest cost and pay off in labour.

Barnardo offered a system of bonuses for energetic effort and scheduled the homesteaders progress. The first few months he would work on his own homestead then he would be employed with his team on the Home Farm with the exception of the time needed to backset his homestead land. The first term, the settler was expected to winter, drawing on his capital for the keep of his oxen in the Farm Home. The second spring, additional outfitting was required and likely he would be supporting two persons, himself and a Barnardo Boy or a wife.

Once the Barnardo settler was established on the land, correspondence was maintained through the *Ups and Downs*.

> Dear Sir:
> This year I shall break 15 acres, and next I shall backset ten, and harrow and seed it, and if I get a good crop I shall have about 800 dollars, and then I shall be able to have a look at the dear old Youth Labour House. Dr. Barnardo's farm at Russell is not far from me, so I shall also be able to have a look at some of the Youths' Labour lads at work.
>
> W.C.R. North West Teritories

> Dear Sir:
> Well, crops in Elkhorn district are looking fine. .
> I have only seen one bad crop since I came to Manitoba. Mixed farming is good here, but I intend going ranching when I am old enough. Wishing you and everyone connected with the Homes every success."
>
> T.J.W. Elkhorn, Manitoba

The demand for Barnardo boys and girls in Canada's West seemed insatiable. With the forging ahead of the great railway schemes, large areas of magnificently fertile land were opened for

Dr. Barnardo's Receiving and Distributing Home 115 Pacific Avenue, Winnipeg, Manitoba   — W.H. Chapman

Road making on Dr. Barnardo's Industrial Farm
"'Road making here means simply ploughing up the prairie soil, turning it over, and then leaving it to be beaten into hardness."   — Dr. Barnardo, 1891 Manitoba Archives

settlement and a large immigration was anticipated. Mr. Owen noted that "under such circumstances we may expect that the demand for our colonists will increase and if we were required to place five thousand children a year I should anticipate no further difficulty providing for them."

In 1896, Barnardo opened his Winnipeg Receiving and Distributing Home, at 115 Pacific Avenue the gift of R.J. Whitla, a prominent Winnipeg resident. Just before Barnardo received the Winnipeg Home, the Land Commissioner of the Canadian Pacific Railway stated in the *Canadian Gazette,* London, that the Canadian North West suffered from a "famine of women" and English speaking general servants of good morals, who would make good farmers' wives should be immigrated as quickly as possible. If not, young Canadian farmers, now living in isolation would leave for the United States. The Gazette emphasized that "women would give more energy to the now weak and ineffectual effort of lone young farmers."

The *Virden Advance* 1904, stated in "The Manitoba Woman's Burden" that western women were becoming "veritable slaves of their environment. We scarcely hear them complain so conscious are they that it is next to impossible to secure help. Such a state of things is a clog on the progress of the Province. Many men have to abandon farming as a profession because their wives are unequal to the physical strain which the endless duties of a farm house impose upon them."

The great want of the North West was women: women to help women, women to help men.

The C.P.R. and Barnardo's publicized the fact that "In the old country a servant remains a servant, always; but in Canada she becomes mistress of her own home."

Barnardo Girls from Ontario were offered encouragement to seek their fortunes in Canada's West.

To go "where there is space and work and large wages. And," continued the *Ups and Downs,* "(this is confidential, and the girls did not say it themselves, but others told it us), there are many young men out there whose stockings are never or poorly darned, whose bread is soggy and weighty, whose wearing apparel is disjointed and shapeless, and whose hearth is unswept. Outside their home everything is shipshape and prosperity looks out from every acre of land, but it's the inside of the home that bothers them."

Dear Sir:

I took the homestead fever, which I thought was
a good idea. It was fine until my sister left. If she
does not come back you had better send me a young
lady, as I have got to be one of the large farmers around
here. I will stick to it a while longer, as I think that it
is time that I was getting married, so if you know of a
young lady who would suit me, send her along. Well,
I remain one of Dr. Barnardo's Old Boys.

C.A.C. Biggar, Sask.

In 1900 Dr. Barnardo visited the West for the last time. From
the Industrial Farm at Russell he wrote his wife:

"You would be charmed with the prospect here.
It is simply lovely from every point of view. The place
is in beautiful order; and my good representative Mr.
E.A. Struthers, has, I think, won the universal respect
of the whole locality."

In 1908, three years after Dr. Barnardo's death, the Industrial
Farm at Russell was shut down. Both E.A. Struthers and A.B. Owen
felt that the Winnipeg Home which had moved to Bannerman
Avenue would serve as a receiving and distributing Home for all
Barnardo Children into Canada's West. Thousands of dependent
boys and girls from over crowded cities had been given new hope and
opportunity in Canada's West. Like most immigrants they arrived
as paupers but rose to become Canada's successful prairie farmers,
industrialists, and professionals. To-day their descendants mold
and guide the nation that opened its great fertile spaces to their
forebearers who came as frightened children trembling into the
bountiful arms of the New World.

PART V

"Canada is a good country. It is freedom, freedom of speech, of resources, freedom of what you may do yourself."

Ups and Downs, 1914

BARNARDO CHILDREN
RECALL

STEPNEY CAUSEWAY, BARNARDO'S "EXPORT EMPORIUM"

It all started with dreams of a trolley ride through London. Now, it was coming true! Never realizing the significance nor the traumatic shock it would be.

That afternoon mom took my hand and we started off. What a thrill! It seems like yesterday. Such ecstasy, I drank in every minute of it hoping it would never end. Then I looked up into my mother's eyes and saw tears. I couldn't understand why mother was crying when I was so happy. She wiped her cheeks as the trolley man told us it was time to get off. Mother and I walked towards this big old house that looked like some kind of a castle to me. We climbed up the steps towards great big double front doors. Mother knocked. The door opened and there stood a gentleman. He invited us to come in. My mother held my hand ever so tight and we went inside. Mother talked with the man and when they were finished she said to me, "Ralph, you go with this man because this is going to be your home from now on." I cried and screamed and kicked. They put me in a room by myself until I stopped. Then one day I tried to run away and find my mother but I never could find her. You see, my mother had 9 children and father, a wharf foreman, died at the age of 42 of a heart attack and one by one mother had to part with us all leaving us with Dr. Barnardo. I was in the home 2 or 3 years and then I was told I was coming to Canada. They showed us pictures of this beautiful land and soon I was on a boat, the S.S. Sicilian, with a wooden trunk with my name on it. In Canada, having my share of ups and downs I became successful and happy and being very gregarious as was my benefactor, Dr. Barnardo, I was one of the first Canadians to take the "Dale Carnegie Human Relations Course."

Ralph Baxter

❖

1903

They took me in and I had a little blue muffler and coat. I was six and I was crying. They sent me to the Girls' Village Home, a beautiful place with rows and rows of cottages each named after a flower. My cottage was Honey Suckle Cottage. After that I went to be boarded out at Aunt Patti's who got paid for keeping us Barnardo Children and sending us to school each day. One day they took me from her and sent me and some other girls to Stepney Causeway where they fitted us for Canada.

Mr. A.B. Owen, the head Canadian man came to get us. We were so excited to get a ride on the boat that we didn't worry much. As we came close to the Canadian shoreline the trees were splendid with colour and I remember saying, "Do trees grow like this in Canada?" I was ten years old. We arrived in Montreal and I can remember sitting on the floor in the Montreal Station, our bags scattered all around us. Finally, we arrived in Peterborough. We had trunks with our full name and number on the front and in the trunk we had clothes, a Bible, a Sankey Hymn Book and a toy.

First, they placed me out at a farm and by 12 years old I had matured into young womanhood which frightened me terribly having no knowledge of it. My periods stopped and the farm woman accused me of playing around with the hired boy as we worked in the fields side by side. She took me to the village doctor and sent me back to Hazelbrae complaining that there was something physically wrong with me.. The Hazelbrae doctor prescribed medicine and soon things were back to normal.

Out I went again, this time I stayed only 2 months and took down with rheumatism and the doctor said I was in a very run down condition so they sent me back to the Home where I stayed for a year to get built up. My nerves were so bad since childhood that bed wetting was an embarrassing problem. In England we were punished for bed wetting and at the Home in Peterborough I had to stand in the hallway while all the children filed past. I hid my face in my pinafore for shame. When I was older the doctor attending me traced my problem back to the childhood punishments and severe nervous condition which had developed. My condition was so run down that I remember one farm woman rubbing my cheeks to get them rosy before the visiting lady from the Home arrived.

Finally they sent me to a maiden lady and her mother where I stayed for 15 years. The woman had to work in the woolen mill to support herself and her mother. The burdochs had grown right to her back door. Each day, I would take the sickel and work the burdochs back. Then I dug a small garden patch further back each year until finally Miss___ had a man plough it. I loved to cut the wood with a cross cut saw securing the log with my foot, whistling away, happy as a lark. I guess I would have stayed there forever, except one day a friend came to me and said: "Listen, are you going to stay with Miss___ all your life? You come out and get a place of your own. In fact I know a place for you at Dr. and Mrs.___."

At the doctor's I was treated like a maid for the first time in my life. I lived in back quarters and used back stairs and was never premitted to be with them. For weeks I would return to my room and cry and write to Miss___. But I could not go back.

Often I thought about Hazelbrae, those big trees and the wide meadow and the hill we used to roll down and the Christmas I stayed, the splendid dinner, Christmas pudding and everything. Even the ladies came and ate with us. On the 24th of May and holidays the Home would have a party out on the large lawn under the trees, we would have tea together. Sometimes Old Girls would come back to the Home to renew acquaintances.

I never heard about or from my own people. Finally I sent to Somerset House to see if I'd been registered and I found out from them that my father was registered as a travelling jeweller and died when I was one year old leaving two brothers and my mother who remarried. I wondered about my mother and Barnardo's said that they were very sorry but she had never inquired for me since she took me to Stepney Causeway.

Alice Rutty Griffin

———⊶══◆══⊷———

1909

My father was employed by "Home and Colonial" where they sold tea, butter and cheese. He was Manager most of his life and belonged to the Methodist Church. Our home life was very happy and I remember in the evenings mother sewing, father reading and we children drawing. But father got very sick and ended up in the sanatorium. A lady offered to take three of us children into the Barnardo Homes, so we were entered at the "Ever Open Door." Father died. Baby brother David was sent to Dr. Barnardo's Babies' Castle. I was in the Girls' Garden Village and I did not like the "Mother" so I volunteered for Canada. I knew I would never get out, because very few parents would ever be able to get better off and pay for their children to come out of Barnardo's. So, I liked to travel and one way out was Canada!

On the trip over in the Sicilian, we had to take on extra cargo at the Le Havre where the gendarmes walked up and down and our Barnardo Boys helped with loading some cargo. After a long time we arrived at Hazelbrae.

My first assignment was at a minister's house. I did not like his wife. She told me all Barnardo Children came from the slums and I replied that I had had as good a home as she. She did not send me back to Hazelbrae but sent me to a farmer down the road where I was happy. One year, the Barnardo Home brought my Mother and little brother David out to Canada. At first mom worked in a factory at $3 a week but my sisters and I left domestic employment and worked in a box factory to pay mother's board. Then mom was able to stay at home and care for our little brother, David.

I married a Barnardo Home boy who was poorly treated on his Canadian farm but we managed on our own and raised a fine family. My little brother David, who was once in Dr. Barnardo's Babies' Castle, died a short time ago and he was considered one of Canada's best radio hams.

Edith Hutchinson

1910

One day I was walking by a house in London, England and someone called: "Wanna go to Canada?"

"Where?"

"Canada."

"When?"

"Next month."

"O.K."

So I entered Dr. Barnardo's and on March 10th, 1910, age 14, I left England for Canada.

In Canada I was in and out of farms all the time. At one farm I accidently let the pigs out on Sunday. I got a terrible beating with a buggy whip. So I wrote to the Home and they sent me a ticket to go back to the Toronto Home. Later, Mr. Owen got a letter from that farmer asking for another Home boy. He asked me, "Does this man deserve another Home boy?" "No, sir," I answered.

Then I went to another farm. I was there three years. The man was always cranky and fighting at the dinner table. One day he tossed his fork at me. It just missed my ear.

On Sundays the Barnardo boys would see each other at church. This one Sunday John went to talk to Billy. The farmer grabbed him and told him that he was not to talk to him. John said, "I'm a Home Boy and so is Billy and if we can't talk then there's going to be trouble." That week Billy hanged himself and Johnnie was found on the stable floor, his stomach full of strychnine.

And then there was Fred. He came to church and later they found him still in his Sunday clothes drowned in the river.

I was sick a lot in Canada. I liked to go back to the Barnardo Home on Jarvis St. where we could do what we liked, play and have fun. Once I was put in the hospital which was in the attic. Mr. Owen examined my swollen, itchy feet and kept me there for a week.

When I was older and on my own I went back to visit the Jarvis St. Home. I knocked and the door was opened by a nun. Another one stood in the hallway behind her. Holy God, Barnardo's had become a Nun's Home! I got out of there.

Hugh Caesar

*Barnardo Girls and Miss Kennedy arriving in Canada from
Great Britain   — Centennial Museum, Peterborough*

*Barnardo Girls at Hazelbrae convalescing or waiting for suit-
able placement   — Centennial Museum, Peterborough*

We were a family of 4 girls and 1 boy. My father passed away and my mother was in poor health. One day a Gentleman came to see my mother and gave her a paper to read. Mother could neither read nor write. He asked her to sign the paper which she did with an X. A few days later my sister and I were at school and we were called out by this Gentleman who told us his name was Mr. Neil from the Barnardo Home in Birmingham and that we were going with him. Mr. Neil got our coats and took us to the train.

Our uniforms were grey dresses and our coats were red with red hats. We were all dressed alike. We were there sometime until some of us were picked to go to Stepney Causeway. We were chosen. Then we were put on a train and sent to Barkingside, the Girls' Village where there were 10 girls to a cottage with a mistress to look after us. The older girls had to do some cleaning and make the beds. We were used really good.

Up to now Marie and I had never been separated but before we were picked out to go to Canada, Marie took very ill and had to go to the hospital. That separated us.

I came to Canada October 1, 1910 on the S.S. Sicilian. There were 150 boys and 150 girls. But something went wrong on board ship and we sailed to France where they let us off the ship but we were not allowed to leave the dock. Back on the ship we had something to eat and a concert. At last we docked at Quebec and we were put on a train, the boys going to Jarvis Street, Toronto and the girls going to Peterborough.

My first placement was in the Muskoka area. I was there several years and the people used me like their own. I kept up with them until they passed away a few years ago. They received $5 a month for our keep.

I had been in Canada five years, never hearing a word about my sister, when all of a sudden Mr. Neil of Barnardo's told me that she was coming to Canada. What joy!

Finally when I got married to a Canadian boy we returned to England and had a wonderful family reunion with my family. We had so much to talk about.

Dolly Griffin

Let me tell you.   In those days people could insure children's lives. Waifs were picked off the street, insured, and when they died the monies were collected.

That's what almost happened to me.   I found myself in a cold dirty room with a pile of straw for a bed.   There was a wash basin with cold water and a dirty rag.   A pail sat in the corner for urinating.   I was locked in there never seeing anyone.   Once or twice a day the door would unlock, a hand would slide through a piece of hard bread and a tin of water.

Finally I got desperate.   I pulled an old box over to the tiny dirty window and looked out into a back alley, garbage piled high. Then I saw a bobby, and he just stood there staring up.   I grabbed my shoe and banged at the window, smashing it to bits.

The authorities found 8 girls and some boys.   My brother was one of them.   So we were put in Dr. Barnardo's Home and in a while I was put out in my first placement.   There they had a daughter my age who used to steal and I'd get the whipping.   One day, alone in the house, sitting by the hearth a spark landed on the back of my dress and I ran out screaming.   A lovely lady found me and rolled me in a mat to smother the flames.   In taking off my charred clothes she was startled to see the whip marks and asked me what happened.   I told her.   She took me to her home and notified the Home.

One Christmas a wonderful vision came to me.   What I saw I shall never forget.   It was God with a rod and staff and two angels who stayed and sang, "God will take care of you".   I wanted to share it with someone, so I told the woman of the house.   She laughed at me and said, "You're daft."

When I was 8 I was sent back to Dr. Barnardo's Girls' Village where I was trained in Housekeeping.   Then I was sent to Canada. We arrived at Peterborough around midnight.   At the Home they checked our hair, our teeth, and our eyes.   After a bath, we assembled for a bowl of soup and the rules were read.   There were about 60 of us and we were marched into the large dormitories and told which bed to sleep in.   Soon the girls stopped crying and fell asleep. Next morning they gave us an extra hour of sleep, then up, washed, dressed and marched down the stairs each to her own particular place.   After the breakfast, each girl got a chore: make the beds, sweep the floor, gather dishes and wash, and scrub the tables and benches.

Well, there was one of the staff with whom I did not get along. It had been rumoured that she had once been a Barnardo Girl, had jumped out a window escaping from a bad home and broken her leg. This day I was cleaning away and singing along. She limps over and tells me to quit the singing and the tables weren't done well enough. So I slopped the cloth across the table again and she slopped the wet cloth across my face. Well I got 24 hour solitary confinement.

I was not happy in my placements. The first place the son on the farm tried to take advantage of me and I fought him off and slapped him. The next place I just got tired of being their slave. So back to the Home.

At Hazelbrae Miss Taylor, the head lady, gave me special duties which were to answer the doorbell, take letters to be signed. There were five or six secretaries working for her. I was very happy and didn't mind being called "Miss Taylor's Pet".

Sometimes business men and ladies in fine dresses would arrive at the Home to visit or adopt the girls. One well dressed gentleman wanted to take me but Miss Taylor told him that I was her own girl. I stayed with this gentle-hearted, white haired lady for 4 months. Then I was placed on a farm with a fine couple who had no children. When I arrived there they had a Barnardo boy who was very tiny in build but ten years older. I took to the farm and farm work right away. The lad became jealous and left. He was 21 and enrolled in the Bantam Patrol.

By 13 I could do a man's work. I was a very willing worker and did the job without hesitation.

Soon I was calling the farmer and his wife, Dad and Mom. Well, Dad took sick with the shingles and his brother came to help me with the farm work. I wept when we had to sell the farm, but at least I was still with my "Dad and Mom."

Mary Warriner

1912

This is my sister. Just the two of us came to Canada. Those are my brothers. They never came to Canada. This is what I held against my mother. I said, "Why send two little girls when two boys could fight for themselves even if they were younger?"

In Canada my sister and I went to a Free Methodist minister's home. The minister's wife played favourites to my younger sister and I was sent by Barnardo's to another farm. The other farm was way off in some distant, cold spot and I had to quit school. I was ready for High School in England, but when I came to Canada they stuck me in the "Aa Bu Kuk" and I played hookey. I wasn't going back to that, so over the foot of the bed with a strap and buckle. I got more beatings in Canada than I ever got. I was punished for things I didn't know what for sometimes. One spring we were rounding up the cattle and the cattle didn't get in the right place between me and the farmer. He took the bamboo rod to me, not only then, but several times. I have a spine injury and I blame it on that man.

The places where some of us Barnardo children have stayed have been rough. Many times I would come in from working in the fields or barn and go to bed with my clothes and all on. And the man's child slept with me and him trying to get into the bed with me and him putting his hand over my mouth so I couldn't yell, and his little daughter right there sleeping. I fought. There was no way.

I've often said that if I'd been left in the position that my mother had been left in I would never have sent two little girls across the sea to a strange land. If I had had four children and no way to support them I would have slit their throats and mine before I'd let them suffer the heartbreak and the loneliness that I've known.

name withheld

I wrote and told my mother I was going to Canada (our letters were censored) and I was told to write another letter and not to mention going to Canada. The night before we got on board the ship we were told we could write a loving letter home. I guess it didn't matter what we said as we would be on the sea when the word was received by mother.

We had a nice trip over, made it in 12 days. The first two days we were all seasick. After that we enjoyed it. The other passengers

The Girls' Distributing Centre, Hazelbrae, Peterborough,
1891   *— Public Archives, Canada*

were all very nice and played games with us and I remember they
turned the skipping rope for us. Our part of the ship was parti-
tioned off from the other passengers.

In Canada somebody by the name of Cox had loaned or
donated a house on Barnardo Street. There were three stories
built on the back of the house for us children. The first floor had
only tables and benches in it. It was the only place we had to live
as the other two floors were full of little cots on which we slept.
These were placed so close together we hardly had room to get into
bed. The original house was used by the staff. The meals consisted
of the same fare each day. Breakfast was oatmeal, and cocoa.
Lunch was vegetable soup and tea was bread and jam or bread
drippings and cocoa. On Sunday we received some bread pudding.
After breakfast, Miss Simpson, the Matron, came in and we had
prayers. The older girls were then sent to various duties such as
cooking, laundry, cleaning and serving the meals to staff. The rest
of us were divided between the two staff Miss Carter and Miss

Pearson. Miss Carter was very nice and we all hoped each day that we would be lucky enough to come under her direction. I did hear a story that Miss Pearson had been a Home Girl and had tried to run away by jumping out of a window, breaking her leg in the attempt. She was lame and wore a boot with a thick sole.

I was sent to my first place in Whitby on October 5, 1912. I believe the Home paid them five dollars a month for my keep until I was 12 years old. I was to go to school until I was 14. I was sent back to the Home when I was 12 and the people got a younger girl. They did the same with the boys they received. I have often wondered why the Home staff allowed this to happen.

We were not allowed in the main part of the house in the Whitby placement, only the kitchen and where we slept. I shared a room over the kitchen with the other girl and the boy had a room at the front of the house. Even though there was a bathroom in the house we were never allowed to use it. We bathed in the kitchen in a wash tub and used the outhouse. We ate in the kitchen, alone.

There were chickens, but we never had an egg. There were two cows but we never had butter. There were pigs and at Christmas time pork was the only meat we had.

In June 1913, I was very sick. The doctor made all arrangements for my trip to Toronto. He called the station to check train time. The police met me at the train and took me to the hospital. I had a constrictive band around the bowel which I had been born with. Then I was refitted at the Home in preparation for being sent to another placement. I overheard Miss Simpson, the Matron, telling the 2 ladies who were sewing clothing "you wouldn't think this girl was lazy."

When I was 18, I was advised by the Home that I was on my own. I came directly to Toronto. I have had my troubles since I have been "on my own" but, I have been much happier. My daughter was born in 1930 during the depression. It was a hard time, but I made sure she didn't get treated the way I had been. She has grown up a very good and well respected girl. She has worked since she was 14 years old and has obtained her B.A. at the University. I am proud of my daughter.

Helen Gough

1914

I was born in Dublin and was spirited out of Ireland where my mother registered my birth in London. She died two years later and I found myself at the mercy of two people I called "Aunt and Uncle". They treated me cruelly and I took to the streets hunting for orange and apple peels left in the gutters. Sometimes I would sit at my favourite spot where on clear days I could see the cathedral at Newmarket. One day as I was strolling along the streets I was picked up to be sent to Canada.

The ship was called the Corinthian. The date was September 10th, 1914 and the North Sea was peppered with German submarines. I was 11 years old and terrified. This ship sailing back was renamed the Morinia and many Barnardo boys who had joined the army sailed back on the troop ship which had brought we hundred of children to Canada. We'd met a boatload of soldiers on their way over. The ship blew its whistle and we waved at the soldiers.

Then onto the "Barnardo Special". The train passed through orchard country and the trees were filled with the biggest, red apples I had ever seen. This was Canada!

The first farm I went to, I stayed for 10 fine years, as hired man. This farm I loved. They had 70-80 hogs, 14 horses. At Christmas we sold baby beef and ate oysters and goose for dinner. All the livestock were "mine". I even got to take the horses to the local Fair and the Boss took me to the Toronto Exhibition and we'd drop in at 50-52 Peter St., Dr. Barnardo's Headquarters. It hurt me not to be given a special welcome but they had so many cases to deal with. Boys were poorly treated by many farmers who worked the head off the kids even using whips and pitch forks.

One year a Barnardo Musical Corp came to Canada and put on a concert at Stratford. Well, were they splendid, ringing those hand bells all dressed in smart sailor suits with white collars! Barnardo's encouraged music and after that concert my boss let me take up the fiddle.

One Sunday while reading the Barnardo publication *Ups and Downs,* I got the surprise of my life to see that my older brother had come to Canada 2 years before and was living on a farm only 15 miles away from me!

Well, after we served our term as Barnardo boys we both got itchy feet and took to the road travelling across this great country, always finding work on the railway, in road construction, harvesting, lumbering. We were happy. Canada was God's country!

C. W.

I was an orphan child. I have no recollection of my parents, whatsoever. I was placed with Aunt Ellen, a spinster lady, who made her living by keeping Dr. Barnardo's children, and I was one of them. I stayed with Aunt Ellen eight years and went to school close by.

Now, in England, there was the upper class and the lower class. The rich were ordered by council to save all their scraps such as dried crusts and stale cake for us poor folk. I would walk to the clergyman's house with the wicker basket and the servant girl would fill it. Aunt Ellen picked it over very carefully and made delicious bread pudding. Well can I remember Aunt Ellen having to divide an egg among the three of us and on Easter morning was a whole hen's egg each!

Sometimes we would walk in the meadows where the flowers grew and red poppies blew in the wind. We would climb over stiles and hear the cuckcoo call its mate.

Now September, 1914 had arrived and so had my time to leave Aunt Ellen and England. It broke my heart. I cried and cried. I couldn't eat or sleep. I went to say good-bye to my school mates. "Don't go, don't go! The ship will go down like the Titanic." They begged me not to go to Canada, reminding me of the slides we had seen on the Titanic.

The next morning I walked to the train. The conductor lifted me on as I was unwilling to leave the only mother I ever knew. So now, along with other sad children we headed into Stepney Causeway, London where each of us was tagged with our names and a number.

Within a few days, we boarded the train for Liverpool where we received four innoculations. Then up the gang plank and onto the Corinthian. We were now leaving the shores of dear old England and sailing the high sees for Canada. For two weeks all we saw was water and then icebergs. But one day, we girls did see something! We were called on deck, a submarine was sailing along side our ship.

It would remain on the surface for a time then submerge and we were told that due to the outbreak of the war this submarine was for our protection. The thought of the Titanic came to my mind but we were given encouragement to erase any disaster from our young minds. From our cabin down below, we would look out through the port holes and see the high waves dashing and splashing. When we were eating our soup or Irish stew, the food would sway to and fro. Many of us were sea sick which made lots of work for the ship's stewards.

After about 14 days of sailing, we were told that the ship was going down the great St. Lawrence River and we could see the Canadian shoreline. Then we boarded a train and the boys went to Jarvis Street, Toronto and the girls went to Peterborough.

My stay at Hazelbrae was short. One morning the Matron called me to the office and told me that I would be going to Garden Hill. So, my morning arrived. I once more boarded the train and I was given another box lunch. I still had my tag with name and number fastened to me and off I went with two other Barnardo Girls.

At the Garden Hill Station the station agent looked after me until a buggy arrived with a tall, very sober faced youth. He told me to get into the buggy and took me to my first Canadian home. I was ushered to my bedroom along with my Barnardo trunk and saw inside for the first time. In it there was a lovely wardrobe: two sets of winter under wear, dresses, aprons, boots, stockings as well as new summer clothing. The contents of the trunk served as a tonic in a strange land.

I went to school until I had to stop at age fourteen as I went on wages at $8 to $10 per month. My mind used to meditate on being a nurse or teacher as I knew I had the mental capacity but no opportunity. My foster parents received good board money for me.

One Christmas I had no money to buy a present for a classmate. She thought herself very superior to most of us especially to me, a Barnardo Girl. I thought and thought what I could give her and finally I gave her my treasured book out of my Barnardo trunk. My first Christmas in Canada I was eight years old. No one told me to hang up a stocking as dear Aunt Ellen had said but I did anyway. In the morning it was empty! But the dear foster male parent slipped out to someplace and brought me back a lovely doll in white slippers. But the wife, she was mean and ruled us with an iron hand.

Garden Hill: One of the hundreds of Canadian depots that received Barnardo Children

— Courtesy John Long Collection

Before leaving for Canada Barnardo's proteges perform for their patron Queen Victoria in the Royal Albert Hall

— Barnardo Archives

Even when the visiting lady would visit me every six months I never complained about this woman. I wouldn't dare complain for this foster woman would drill into me that I would be severely punished.

On October 2, 1925 the house was burned to the ground. The day was extremely hot and four of us had been working in the fields hauling in turnips. I was sent to the pasture to bring in the cows and the wife was to check the oven fire where bread was baking. Instead she stayed outside and when I came up the lane with the cows smoke was ascending from the house. I ran inside and tried to salvage my personal souvenirs. My Barnardo trunk was nothing but twisted metal and we were left with nothing but our work clothes on our backs and were cast on the neighbours for mercy and I, the Barnardo Girl was blamed for the fire! The community did not believe a word of the accusation. I should have left them but I stayed and helped them build a new home helping with barn chores as well as carrying bricks and mortar. I drudged away like their slave. All without wages. Finally the kind foster male parent died. I married and my husband insisted that I be paid my back wages. I asked for $50. The woman made me sign a receipt "paid in full."

When one is young the memory bank stays very clear and permanent. Fond memories and disappointments are retained throughout one's life. Doctor Barnardo was truly a humanitarian caring for the largest family on record. Although strife still exists the younger generations have erased much of this superior nonsense which rebuffed child emigrants.

Daisy Peacock

⸻※⸻

Father died in W.W.I. and mother remarried but my step-father was mean to me and mother had to put me in Dr. Barnardo's. I don't think she knew that I would be leaving for Canada! I liked Dr. Barnardo's and Queen Victoria visited us at the Girls' Village. On special occasions we went to the Royal Albert Hall and played games around the Maypole.

Well, finally I came to Canada and the second farm I stayed at was Catholic. They made me go to church and the woman said I had to learn the Rosary before she would give me anything to eat. That night I ran away and came back to Hazelbrae. Then I was placed on a farm near Orangeville and for five years I was treated badly. Every time Barnardo's visiting lady would come I was sent to my room. The hired man finally wrote the Home and the visiting lady took me to the hospital. I gave her letters to mail to my mother and she never did. I would love to have been with my mother.

Finally, I was placed on a good farm and from there I was married. To-day I have 18 grandchildren and 15 great-grandchildren. I wouldn't want to live the first part of my life over again but after my marriage life got much better.

Annie Hall (Richmond)

1915

I didn't want to go in to Stepney Causeway and my step mother and I both stood there and cried. The matron told us to go home and be reconciled and come back. So she brought me back again and they took me into this room that was full of dolls, big dolls, little dolls, all kinds of dolls. They gave me the biggest doll and said that I should be very happy because it was the matron's doll. But I was very upset and very young and very unhappy.

Barnardo's placed me out in England and the vicar's wife knew what was happening to me so I went back to the Girl's Village, Barkingside where I stayed with twenty other girls in a cottage called James Tyler. Every morning I was in charge of seven little girls. We had a fine educational system and I was in the choir and we sang at the Royal Albert Hall.

I shall always remember when I was 15 this lady and gentleman came to the school and the lady turned to her husband and said, "There's Doreen and she hungers for love." The couple was Mr. and Mrs. John Hobday, from the Canadian Headquarters. We were going to Canada and they gathered us into a large group and told us what was expected.

"You are going out into a new country and you
are British subjects and you are to show the people
in Canada that you are a good subject. It is your

duty to prove yourself to the Canadians, especially
to the Canadian government because it was they who
were interested in having the young people come out.
If you don't do well the government will not have that
class of young person come over. It is your life, you
know what is right and wrong."

We arrived in Canada. The boys went to Toronto and the girls to Peterborough. It was a lovely house, Hazelbrae, and we were met by a lovely middle aged lady. We didn't stay there long but were placed-out.

My first place was a Scottish minister's. He was a typical Scotsman demanding more than I could give. Then I went to a private school. They really wanted someone who could manage the whole household as well as the children.

Back at the Home I expressed the thought that these Canadians were expecting more of me than the British. Perhaps I didn't understand their ways. The Canadian Home told us:

"Now, you are in Canada and you must learn to
do what Canadians do. Don't say, 'Well we do it
like this in England'. You must learn the Canadian
way."

But my real complaint lay hidden: Canadians just wanted to use me as a scullery-maid.

At 21 I was no longer under Barnardo's care. I had made up my mind that I wasn't going to do this type of work all my life.

I had carefully banked all my money and was determined to be a nurse. I applied to the Cornwall General Hospital and went in for a personal interview. The Superintendent asked me where I stayed and what was my education. She couldn't compare the English and Canadian education but she said: "That isn't worrying me a bit. The minute you walked through the door, I knew I was going to accept you."

I graduated as a Registered Nurse and four years later married a wonderful man. Mrs. Rose Hobday, the Lady Superintendent of Barnardo's Canada with whom I maintained contact was godmother to my eldest daughter.

I have three daughters and sometimes my son thinks that I over indulge them but I always look back and say, no, they have everything I should have had.

                                                    Doris Frayne

1916

From the time we left the Home in England all kindness stopped. We were on our own, I never knew what profanity was or what a beating was until I was on that first Canadian farm.

When I arrived on the first farm, the cattle were in the orchard. I had never seen cattle before. I was told to drive the cattle out. I thought back to England where you'd see at the crossroads an arm pointing one way and another the other way. So I stood there facing the cows, one arm one way, the other the other way towards the gate. The woman was watching and she nearly died.

It didn't take me long to learn and soon I was up at 4:30 each morning to get the cows back to the barn before daylight. One morning I didn't get them down there on time and the farmer hid behind the barn and grabbed me. He had a huge strap. I got the buckle end of that strap for a good 5 minutes. It's an agony that I'll never forget. This same man also rubbed my face in cow manure. One day he had bothered me so terribly that I couldn't stop crying. He threatened to knock me with a shovel unless I stopped. Next I worked for a religionist. He was one of the worst. He was supposed to be a Christian and he was anything but. At this time I wasn't feeling well. I did my best. He complained to the home that I was lazy, which was an absolute lie. He had my wage deducted from $100 a year which I was to get at age 14 down to $45. Then he decided to beat me up when I wasn't feeling up to it. He knew how to beat people up. And I did my best there.

Those are old memories and they kind of get to you.

In my Barnardo trunk I had a yellow and green silk tie brand new from Dr. Barnardo and the farm woman grabs into the trunk and says, "We'll fix that!", and tied it on for a garter.

I sure grew out of my clothing fast and this farmer would not buy me any. I was all the time pulling my britches down to meet my stockings so I could hide my underwear. And the farmer would stand on the veranda and shout at me as far as he could see me.

Another place they sent me I would much rather have spent the 2 years in jail. I had to wheel the manure up from 60 cattle and 20 head of horses. I was forever on the end of that delapidated old wheel barrow. Once I was ploughing and the handle broke off the plough and the plough rolled upside down. He kicked me across a sixteen acre field. I'd just get half way to my feet and he'd kick me again sending me sprawling into the dirt. He beat me unmercifully. Once he took a club to me. I ran like mad and crawled away in the dark.

Old memories die hard. Some guys say you ought to go back and clean up on them but that doesn't make sense. One builds up a distinct dislike for these kind of people and it's hard to erase the meanness from your memory. When I look back on my childhood I say to my own children, "Give your children the happiest childhood you can because it's a memory they will not forget."

Len Russell

1920

I do not remember my father. I cannot remember what my mother looked like but to this day I can hear my mother screaming with pain in her room. I wanted to go in to see her but they would not let me go in. She died a few days later.

Then my sister took over looking after the house and she worked hard to keep us looked after. How I loved the bread pudding she would make! After school I would come home and grab a big hunk of her pudding and go out to play. Nobody worried about where I was as long as I got home at supper. My sister did not worry. I always got some farmer's apples or got into his field of swedes.

The split up of the family came when my two oldest brothers got married. Well, with my brother's wife things had to change. I had to be home on time for meals and I was not to go off the street. But to me I could not change that fast. I would ramble away in the mountains and hills of Wales and all time was lost to me.

I would come home late for tea and she would beat me and send me to bed without anything to eat. I was beaten so many times I got used to it.

So one day after being beaten and sent to bed, my brother and his wife went out. I was in bed in my room when this lady (God bless her, I wish I could thank her today but I guess she is long gone and if there is a Heaven I am sure she is there) came into my room with a tray full of eats and told me to eat it all up and not leave one crumb around. That I sure did.

The next day, two men came to the house. They had uniforms on but I don't think they were policemen. They stripped me down and could see how I had been beaten. I was taken from my brother and his wife to a small home in Cardiff, Wales not too far from my old home before the family split up.

Well, I was there one month, then I was sent to a home in London, England. It was called the "Ever Open Door." O boy! was that the place! It was a small home and I was used good. I had a free hand there too as long as I came home at the time I was told to, which I did. If I wanted to go to a picture show the master of the home would give me a pass card and all I had to do was show it at the picture show door and I got in. Then he got me a job at the swimming baths, gathering all the towels and bathing suits in both the men's and ladies' swimming baths. O boy! I guess they figured I was harmless at 11 years old. They used to throw money in the swimming pool and I would dive for it. Well, that lasted for about two months. I sure hated to leave that place.

I was taken to another place in London called Stepney Causeway. There were about 200 boys there. It was a big place. The yard had a high wall around it. To me it was a jail, no way out. Some of the boys would climb the wall at night and run away but they were always caught and brought back and then they would get a terrrible thrashing for their trouble. I did not want that so I behaved myself. The place had a large room on the ground floor with long tables and benches which I learned later was the boys' eating place. The floor above was a large bedroom. There were about 300 single beds in it. The floor was so shiny you could see your face in it and I soon found out how they got it that way. Every morning before daylight and before breakfast, that large dormitory had to be swept, dusted and floor polished. One lot of boys would start the sweeping and dusting and about ten boys would line up on their hands and knees and put the polish to the floor. Then another row of boys, me too, would follow up on our hands and kneess with polishing cloths and we had to rub that floor so you could see your face in it. Life at Stepney Causeway was firm, you did as you were told. But on Saturdays we were taken to Clappen Commons which was a big park. We had sports, football and baseball. It was all under supervision because that was when some of the boys took their chance to run away. The schooling we got was at the home. We also had boxing matches.

The first thing I was asked when I got with all the boys. "Can you fight, boy?" I began to think this was a place where you had to stand up for yourself or get knocked down. So the day came for the boxing contest.

There were three brothers. Their names were Smarts (their first names I do not recall) but they were the bullies of the home. All the boys were afraid of them. So one of them got in the ring but no one would take him on. So me being new I said I would take one. I put the gloves on and we into it and fists were flying. As he ducked to miss my punch I came up with a punch under the chin and I floored him. O boy, the cheers went up. I was the hero of the Home. From then on I had no trouble.

Saturday was bath day for everybody. We would all have to take a hot bath, then right after the hot bath we had to jump into the swimming pool which was cold water. If you did not go in yourself, you got tossed in. Boy, was that a shock but we had to go in!

Sunday was church day. We had all the same clothes. We would all march out of the home through the streets of London to the church. One part of the big church was kept for the home boys and was up in the gallery. We were all one big choir. We could sure raise the roof.

Now comes the first talk of some of us going to Canada. This morning my name was called. Oh, boy, what had I done? There were about 36 of us called up front, and then they dismissed all the rest from the large dining room. So we were all prepared for the worst when we were told we were all picked ot go to Canada if we passed the doctor's O.K. We had to write to our closest relation to get permission to be sent to Canada. So I wrote to my brother Harold to get his permission and I told him he was not to stop me because I wanted to go and to please not stand in my way. Harold sent word back that I could go. I passed the doctor but some did not and I felt sorry for them because the excitement of going to Canada was built up in their hearts.

Well, the day came for us to leave. It was June, 1920. I was 12 years old and it was the biggest day of my life. We were all lined up and the band played the tune of Colonel Bogie and to this day when I hear that being played that day comes back to me. We boys had one verse we use to tune in on that. The saying was "Does your mother chew tobacco like she used to".

Well, we arrived at Liverpool where the boat was waiting for us. It was a small boat. We were all wondering if they were going to send us on that boat. But the small one took us to the larger one that was out in deeper water. There we were beside that big boat wondering how we were going to get up that high. Someone said we would have to go through the port holes. But we soon found out. A ramp was dropped and we all got aboard. What a cheer when we started to sail!

Our trip across was very rough at times. It took ten days on the water. At times it appeared to us as if the boat was going under the big waves but it would raise and ride over the top.

That is when all the sea sickness started. There were 150 boys and 50 girls on the boat. If you did not feel sick you were soon going to be. We had to line up to get washed in the morning. I remember I was in that line up, towel on my arm, when all of a sudden I felt sick. I grabbed my towel and headed for the deck, towel over my mouth. Well, I was greeted by a lot more that had the same trouble and when they say "heave" boy, that I did. I was sick for about two days, then I was O.K. We saw icebergs, lots of them, and passed the spot where the big ship Titanic went down. To us it was a frightening time, going by the icebergs, but we were far enough away from them. We also saw lots of sharks and whales, the water spouting out of their heads. All we hoped for was that the boat would stay on top. They kept us busy with games, entertainment, so we did not get a chance to get homesick.

We were sailing up the St. Lawrence River at night, the lights of the towns were on both sides of us. We landed at Montreal. Then we were put on the train and were all sent different ways. I was sent to Toronto to a home there where a Mr. Hobday was in charge. I was only there a day, then I was put on a train at Toronto to start my journey to where I did not know. I had a tag tied to my coat. I was being sent parcel post. I landed in Ripley, Ontario along Lake Huron. I got off the train where the conductor said I was to get off. The station agent came out and looked at my tag on my coat. O yes, he said, I know who you are for, I will call them and tell them you are here. It must have been harvest time in July, 1920 because the station agent came out and said he was to take me to the hotel because the people I was for were busy and they would be out to pick me up at night. I was there just a little while when I began to realize I was alone in a land I knew nothing about or what was in store for me and I started to cry. I could not stop. The hotel keeper came to me and asked me what was wrong. I said I was homesick and wanted to go home. I guess I figured I would

Barnardo Boys assist at an Ontario thrashing scene
— Ups and Downs

walk home 5000 miles. So the hotel keeper got his boy, who was my age, to take me out in the yard to play ball. That seemed to take my mind off home.

Then came the meeting with the people I was for. He came for me in a horse and buggy. He had bananas and asked me if I wanted one. I sure did for a banana was a real treat for me. He asked me if I had ever been on a farm. I did not know what a farm was.

When we arrived at the farm I met the lady of the house. At my first look at her I knew she was going to be nice. She was kind and gentle.

Well, my days of work started. He told me to go back to the field and bring the cows home. He said, "Have you ever seen a cow?" Of course, I had never. I had heard lots of stories about bulls, that they would chase you if you wore something red. Well, back I go for the cows. I got into the field and there were the cows, about 12 of them. They looked at me with their ears forward. I looked at them, shaking in my boots. To me they all looked like bulls. They started for me and I turned and ran as hard as I could to the barn, crying as I ran. Soon as I got to the barn, I was asked where the cows were. I said they chased me out of the field. He said, "You get back there and go in that field and start yelling your head off and waving your hands and they will come." I made a big circle around them and did just as I was told. They came to the barn for me. Lesson No.1 on cows.

Mrs. M___ was the kindest and most true lady I had ever known, not a harsh word did she say to me. I was there from 1920 to 1926. O yes, she corrected me in many a way in my grammar and things I would say and do but she did it in a way that I respected her. To me she was the only mother I will ever know, never a wrong did she say about anybody, always a kind word. She drilled it into my mind, -now don't smoke or drink, you will be better off and someday you will meet a nice girl and get married. To this day, I have not smoked or drank. She is in her 80's now and he is 90 and I am sure when she goes over that hill the gates will be wide open for the love she gave to others cannot be counted.

Now Mr. M___ I am sure, would not want me to say he was soft and easy to work for. He had to work hard when he was a boy and that was the way he was going to bring me up. I did as I was told, if I liked it or not, or I got told in no mild way. They were only married six months before I went there and times were hard for them but they had the love for one another that won out over any troubles they had. We lived in a log cabin. It was about ¼ mile from the house. In the winter time it was nice and warm, it was low and easy to heat.

Now to tell you some of the training I got. He sent me up to the hay mow to put down hay for the cattle. I could not pull the hay out, it was packed in so hard. I yelled down the hay chute that I could not pull the hay out. Well, he hollered back, "Get down on your hands and knees and pull it out with your teeth." Lesson number one, do it or else find a way.

Farming in those days was a lot harder than now. We were up at 5 o'clock in the morning till 9 or 10 at night. Before I went to school I had to milk cows, clean stables and feed pigs and cattle. I had so much to do before I left for school.

The first three years I was there I got my keep and some schooling. The next three years, my pay was $50.00, the next year $75.00 and the next $100.00 which I got when I was 18 years old and on my own.

A home inspector used to come to the farm while I was there to see if everything was going well with me. His name was Mr. Black. I guess he would talk to Mr. M___ to see if I was doing O.K.

It was a hard life for a boy 12 years old, long hours and hard slugging, everything was done by manual labour. We went to church on Sundays. I used to sit on a little seat between them. No work was done on Sunday, only what had to be done.

We used to get one day off a year. Ripley Fair day was a big day. Mr. M___ would give me 25 cents and he would tell "now don't spend it all, always bring some home and you will never be out of money." Five cents to get in, 5 cents for a ride on something, 5 cents for an ice cream cone and I always came home with a few cents. That was my lesson on how to save.

Well, in the 6 years I learned how to work hard and long hours and you got nothing unless you did work. It was a hard schooling but it paid off in the years ahead.

My one wish all my life was that if I ever got married I would live long enough to see my family married and away from home. I did not want them to go through what I did, when it came that nobody wanted you. Our two girls are married, we have three grand-daughters, and one grandson. Our girls gave us no heartaches, they were both good girls. Our oldest daughter is married to an Armed Forces man. He is a Major and was a Commanding Officer. My youngest girl's husband works for the C.N.R. and they are happy together.

In 1967 my brother Bill and his wife came to Canada to see us. When he saw what we had over here these are his words, "They say over there poor M sent to Canada all on his own, I think it was poor Billy left over in Wales."

I am proud to be a Barnardo Home boy. I do not care who knows it. It's a tough life you had to make on your own but when I look back I feel proud.

Francis M. Williams

1922

Father was reported missing during W.W.1 and my mother was ill for several years so the three of us were placed in Barnardo's in 1919.

In September 1922 one sister and I came to Canada. My mother was bitter about this until her death in 1972. She insisted she never gave permission for our emigration. She died hating the institution. We never saw her after we left England. The preparation for Canada consisted of medical and intelligence tests and fittings for clothes. We had a farewell service at the church and the last farewell to our 8 year old sister. We have never seen her since but do correspond. We all wished the three of us could have come together.

Our ship was the Odanah and we left Southhampton. My first view of Canadian soil was during a vivid sunset and the next day our voyage up the St. Lawrence River was a long lasting memory of blue skies, white waves, ships and clean crisp Canadian air. I was glad to come to Canada. We docked at Quebec where I saw the cliffs of the historical war when France and Britain fought for the title of Canada.

After going through the Department of Immigration at Quebec we were given a box lunch and sent on the train to Montreal where we stopped over at the Old Windsor Station, where we were given a good meal. Then an overnight trip took us to Toronto to the Jarvis Street Home.

The Jarvis Street building was impressive. It must have been very beautiful when it was a family home. Mr. and Mrs. John Hobday, the Superintendents were gentle people and very good looking and they found time to comfort and listen to all. The staff was there to do various chores and we had periods of instruction and moving pictures about Canadian life. We played games in the high walled garden.

In a few days we were moving to our new homes. I was lucky to go to the farm owned by 2 young people and their 2 tiny children. They were hard working people and expected the same of me. They treated me as their own and included me in family gatherings and outings.

To get to school I had to walk across two large farms. My first experience with a Canadian snowstorm was frightening. It happened on the way home from the English Line School. I had to walk across two large farms and if the people hadn't come to meet me I might have been lost. My school teacher and fellow pupils were very kind to me and there was never any snobbery. I corresponded with some for many years.

A year later, age 14, I was sent to various farms as a domestic. Farm jobs were not to my liking. There was always some man try-

A Barnardo Girl as Mother's Helper
— Centennial Museum, Peterborough

ing to make advances towards me. So being a strong minded girl I told the Home visitor I would not work on a farm. This caused me some uncomfortable treatment but finally I was given a place in a small Canadian village which seemed quite normal except for the occasional snobbery towards me because I was a Barnardo girl. But I learned fast how to protect myself. As I was a born leader I became involved in church groups, drama and recreation, often as chairman or President and with such stature I could rebuff the few who chose to be snobbish. I never advertised my Barnardo connection, nobody likes to be a "Home Child", but I am grateful to Barnardo's for bringing me to Canada.

In my 21st year I was no longer a ward of Barnardo's. I met and married a fine man as did my sister. My husband became sick and for 14 years I was breadwinner. The children and I faced poverty, sickness and distress but we all came through stronger people. My children are now grown, all very successful in professions and business and my grandson will soon graduate from law school.

During my life I have contributed to my community and have received the "Canada Medal", the Ontario Horticultural Trillium Award, the International Kiwanis Award, and in 1975 I was chosen as outstanding woman for International Women's Year.

Life has given me many hardships but far more blessings and the Barnardo Home's training gave me strong incentive to get ahead.

Ethel Lewis

My brother George and I were placed in Dr. Barnardo's Home because my parents had a large family to raise. We were in Stepney Causeway for eight months. In the dining room there were long tables and benches. There were so many of us and we were often hungry. We had to clean the floors, make our beds and then we had school lessons. One day they asked if we would like to go to Canada and I said yes, because I was interested in farming.

My mother and Aunt Lizzie came to see us off. On the boat we had a big swimming pool and all the children enjoyed splashing around. As we got near Canada, close to Halifax, we were put on smaller boats to sail to Montreal where trains took us to Toronto, Jarvis Street.

Then off to the Canadian farm. The farmer tied my Barnardo trunk on the back of the buggy. Everything was so strange. I remember going for the cows in the pasture and I was so scared and took the farmer's hand. When I worked at the woodpile, Grandma would bring me cookies in her apron pocket. At breakfast they asked if I wanted cream on my porridge and I wondered what that was. I stayed there five years, paid back part of my ocean passage to Dr. Barnardo's and received a good behavior medal.

When going to school some of the children would say, "Don't play with him, he is a 'Home Boy'." I didn't pay much attention to them. The visitor from the Barnardo Homes would come to the school and they would send the other children outside. I never had to go back to the Homes for sickness or abuse, although some of the children had to attend hearings in Toronto because of maltreatment.

I was really lucky to have a farm home where I was treated like a son, although I was never officially adopted. I worked on the farm with my employer until I was married and I finally bought the farm from the kind family where I had spent my first five years in Canada. Our sons have their own farms and I have lovely grandchildren. I am grateful to Dr. Barnardo's Homes for taking such an interest in the boys and girls of England by bringing them to Canada where they could start rich new lives.

Walter Longyear

I was a lone wolf. I had no father, no mother, no sisters, no brothers. I just dropped.

My first memory is being huddled up in a place where all that hid the bed was a curtain. Then this man, whoever he was, came in drunk ... and my mother ... she must have been my mother ... grabbed me and out she ran. And that is what I remember.

In Canada I was sent to farms. I was worked like the very Sam Scratch himself. And you had to take it. Well, they had one rule that the Barnardo Girl couldn't be left alone on the farm with the hired man. Well, they had gone with the horse and buggy and the visiting lady arrived. She asked, "Do you know who is here on the place?" I said, "Just me and the hired man." I was shipped back to the Peterborough Home for a day or two and out I went again to a farm on an island! The man on the island was a Sunday School Superintendent but was he mean! He wouldn't even let me whistle and milk the cow at the same time. I slept in the attic and often woke with frost on my pillow. The man would beat his horse and raise ridges on its back and he did the same to the hired Barnardo boy. Eventually I said, "To heck with the Barnardo Home. I'm going on my own." And I ran away and they never came to find me. But the Lord looked after me. I married, had my own family and I made up my mind that my children wouldn't go through the life that I went through, and thank God they haven't.

Margaret Wilson

1923

I was born in Islington, Barsbury in the county of London, England. My sister and I were put in the Dr. Barnardo Home in England when she was 6 and I was 4. We were placed by the Home in a foster home where we stayed 8 years. They were nice people but they thought we weren't good enough to eat at the same table with them. We ate on the stair steps with a curtain drew between us and the kitchen. They had 5 children of their own so I guess the money they got for us was to help them out as the Home always provided our clothes.

Every so often a lady would call on us from Dr. Barnardo's to weigh us and she asked us if we were treated right. We daren't say we ate on the stair steps but it always stuck in my memory.

Then when I was 12 and my sister 14 we were taken to the Girls' Village Home where there was a den mother in each cottage. One night they told us we were going to Canada. I cried as we had been at the foster home so long. It was like tearing one from one's own home.

Before we left for Canada our real mother came to see us off. She gave my sister a little jar of cream. I guess it was for both of us.

When we landed in Halifax we were put on a train and sent to Toronto. I was still sick, it was such a long journey to Jarvis St. We stayed there a little while and then my sister and I were separated.

I loved those people so much. They had no children of their own and the lady was sick a lot and I had to help out. Later I went to another place where I worked for $10 a month. The Home used to send someone to check on me every once in a while.

Even when I was first married to the brother of my mistress the Home sent a lady to see how I was doing. One day I was baking bread when she came to the door and she said, "What a lovely aroma!"

Lots of Barnardo Children still won't admit they are Home Boys or Girls because people might snub them. I always had that feeling. But I am glad I came out to Canada and I am not alone today because I now have 42 grandchildren and 8 great-grandchildren, all descendant because I emigrated as a Barnardo Child to Canada.

Louise Stevens

Boys Home, Isle of Jersey. Guild Messenger
— courtesy Harold Green

Our father died and my mother worked at the coal mines in Wales to feed four growing boys. It was too much for her. She died. We were put in Dr. Barnardo's Homes and before sailing for Canada we were taken before three judges to declare that we were going to Canada of our own free will, 99 boys and 21 girls, age 14-15. To the new world we sailed on the Montrose for six wonderful days.

In Canada I worked hard, and then started farming on my own. Then I started working another farm on shares. I was now independent. The Barnardo boys come to live and work with me. Mr. Black, the Barnardo's visiting man whom I liked as a lad, came to visit his boys on my farm. I was Sunday School Superintendent at the local church, sang in the choir and my sons and grandsons followed in my footsteps. I joined the Department of Agriculture as an Inspector. I spent ten years as a school trustee and at present am on the Central Ontario Conservation Authority Board.

Right now I have 22 grandchildren.

Dr. Barnardo's Homes have been very good and I am grateful.

"We thank thee, Lord, for all Thy care
For strength to earn; the chance to share,
For laughter, song and friendships deep
And all the memories we keep."

Edgar A. Guest

Leslie Coombs

Now, as far as the Dr. Barnardo Homes were concerned, they were good, excellent. Our meals were good and our discipline was strict. We had men with canes walking around in the dining hall in order to keep order.

When I was 10 I left England and went to the Dr. Barnardo Home on Jersey Island. The school there was in French and English and we had a very strict superintendent, his name was Captain ___ . The discipline was so strict that we had to protect ourselves. Why I mention this is that we had a boy killed because he stole one tomato from a French farmer. He was not whipped with a strap but he was hit with a bamboo cane and was lashed 18 times. Please do not forget this. Eighteen times is too much for a young boy. Three of the 170 boys watching, grapped him, broke the bamboo cane, and took the lad away. The boy died during the night. This is only one story of what happened. I could give you more than that! This is to give you to understand what we went through the first years in Jersey. We were too small to protect ourselves.

After a while I went back to England to say goodbye to mother. I was going to Canada.

"Canada is a good country. It is freedom, freedom of speech, of resources, freedom of what you may do yourself."

I came to Canada in 1923. The ship I was on had been a war ship that had been captured in the first, great war and had been turned into a passenger. We had 14 girls and 114 boys. In deep water, ½ mile from England, my twin brother was taken off the ship, unknown to me, and returned by Red Cross vessel to England. He was supposed to go to Australia and I to Canada.

Now concerning the farming situation, you may naturally get with a good man or a very poor man. You must understand that the Barnardo Boys were under law to maintain everything the farmer told him to do.

Now ladies and gentlemen I am going to tell you the true facts of the first year that I came out here. The first place no finer people ever lived. But I was only there a week and a half when the farmer sent me back to Jarvis Street saying I was too small to do the heavy work.

My next place was a disaster. Both the woman and man pounded me. She whipped me on my bare arms and legs continually with a willow gad. And the farmer used a horse trace with a chain on the end on my back. For years I carried the marks. My clothing was never anything. I grew out of the breaches and still was made to wear them. I could not take this treatment any longer. This happened in under 5 months, these beatings. One night, after everyone was asleep I wrote a note to the village policeman telling him what was happening to me. I took the note and left it in his mailbox. The policeman informed Barnardo's who requested that the farmer be sent to Toronto for an investigation based on the agreement as to how he was to use and protect his boys when he got them. I was not the only one abused. There were many, many abused in Canada in those years. The farmer had the authority.

After that I worked on several farms where I was happy.

Harold Green

–•–⁓⧓⁓–•–

1931

My father was a Fishmonger in Hammersmith. He died at age 42 years when I was four years old. I remember going to his funeral. I can still see him laying in our front room in his coffin.

My mother carried on with my father's business pushing a fishmonger's barrow around the streets of London selling shell fish such as Winkles, Cockles, Mussells, Shrimp mostly on Sundays, then during the week she would work in the daytime preparing her Barrow to go out at night to the pubs with her wares of Cockles, Mussells and Oysters and would stay till they closed late at night. So that us children were practically left alone most of the time. We were just running the streets. Then one day Mum took me to Fulham Infirmary, which is a kind of hospital. I had my eighth birthday in there on October 5, 1923. I was there a month, there was nothing the matter with me. I was just put there, why, I cannot recall. Then one day a nurse came to the Infirmary and took me away to another place called Parsons Green. This Infirmary was like a Military Hospital and there were a lot of patients from the First World War. I was at this place Parsons Green just a day then my mother came and took me to the Doctor Barnardo's Home, 18 Stepney Causeway. It was foggy and damp, a very depressing day.

I was at Stepney about 2 weeks, 3 days. I remember going through the process of getting ready to go to the first foster home: seeing Doctor Jim Milne, having my picture taken, getting set up with clothes, which were put in a cloth bag about the size of a large pillowcase with my name on front and tied at the neck. This was the beginning of my Foster Home experience. My first place was a little place in Norfolk about five miles from Norwich called Stoke Holy Cross. There was another little boy with me, Stanley, four years old and I was responsible for him. I can remember a lot of unpleasant things while I was there. The discipline at this place was beyond reason. One day the Matron came from the Home in London to see me and check on my health and weigh me. I remember her saying I had gained only a ½ lb. in a year. Well then soon after I was on my way back to Stepney in London.

Then off to another Foster Home. I was there the month of August, 1927. While there the Doctor from Stepney came and examined me. After he had checked me out he said, "How would you like to go in the Navy?" This was the first time anybody had said about going in the Navy so I said yes.

A short time later I was on my way to the Watts Naval School in Norfolk. Watts Naval Training School had 300 boys ages from 11 to 16. It was frightening at first. They called you a 'new cop' and you sure had to be on your toes because in this place you did not go home at night. You were there 24 hours a day, week in and week out, for years sometimes. I was there 3 years and 2 months, and believe me this was some training. As I have looked back over the years I think that training set me up proper, and I was able to cope with my life as it went by without Parental Guidance. While at the school I engaged in all sports, played for my Dormitory, played soccer-cricket for the school against outside teams, excelled in boxing, won a trophy for my dorm three years in a row. A good average student, was in gym class and drill party which gave displays outside in the different towns at special events. I was in top class at Regular Schooling and was good prospect for Al Sailor, well up in Nautical Training.

While at the school I was inflicted with a pain in my hip joint. The doctor diagnosed it as rheumatism. I think this must have been the reason why I was chosen to go to Canada. Doctor Mac-Donald came to the school in the summer of 1930 and I was examined by him. After he was finished, out of the blue he said to me, "How would you like to go to Canada?" Just like that.

While at the school I was able to write to my mother direct which was in 1927. Just before Christmas I was able to go and see her. My mother had to pay my fare to London to get me home for 2 weeks. She did not know me when I got off the train. I was in a sailor's uniform. When I went up to her she asked me if I was Johnny. My mother was still a fishmonger and still doing the same type of work. The times I saw my mother it never occurred to me to ask her why I could not stay home. I think that there was no feeling of belonging there on account of being away so long and in so many different places. It took a little time to realize where I was going, after they told me definitely I was to go. Then on November 4th, 1930 I was sent back to London (Stepney). Another boy from the Watts was with me. Next I was sent to the Liverpool Home on Myrtle Street called the Overseas Training Branch to prepare the boys for going on the farms in Canada. We used to go to the Corporation Stables of Liverpool City to learn about horses and cattle, but we really did not learn that much, not even how to milk a cow.

It seemed like a long time before we went to Canada, 6 months at Liverpool. By that time we were all getting pretty excited about going. We had lectures about it and saw doctors and Canadian Officials. We were all looking forward to it like a great adventure. The clothing that was supplied to us consisted of 2 suits, 2 pair of boots, 2 shirts for work, 2 for best, 1 pair overalls, socks, 1 cap, 1 small trunk and an attache case, a Bible, prayer book, traveller's guide, book called *While We're Young* and a *Pilgrim's Progress*. Then came the big day, Friday, April 10th, 1931 at 3 p.m. we set sail for Canada, aboard the Duchess of Richmond, a 26,000 ton steamer.

On April 18, 1931 we landed at Quebec. We spent one night on the train and arrived in Toronto Union Station early Sunday morning and went to 538 Jarvis Street where Mr. John Hobday greeted us. There was a building at the back of the main house which used to be used as stables years previous and we stayed there until sent to our farms. We had a waving acquaintance with the Nurses across the street in St. Mary's Hospital, and played rounders in the yard. While at Jarvis Street we attended St. Paul's Catherdral, and on Monday went to a show on Yonge Street.

On April 22nd, 1931, Wednesday, we went to the farm by train. When we got to the farm, the farmer helped me carry my trunk upstairs to my room and said to me, "Have you any overalls?" I said, "Yes." He said, "Put them on and go sown to the barn." He was harnessing three horses and we went out to the field and started to harrow it. He said, "I have to go into town", and left me with a team of three horses and the diamond harrows, and said, "Carry on. I will not be long." That was my introduction to the Canadian farm.

I was very disappointed with farm life in Canada, and with the people I worked for. Mr. George Black, the visitor from the Home, came to visit me a couple of times. I told him I was not happy here. One time he came and told me that Billy the Barnardo Boy from Watts, had been killed and said he had fallen off a straw stack and landed on a pitchfork while at a threshing. I cound not believe it. I wanted to see him again more than anybody else and he was gone.

I left the farm. The farmer did not give me any money. I had nothing. I walked from there to Long Branch where I found Bill, my brother. A few days later I walked to Toronto to look for work. I really did not know where I was going but I went anyway.

When I turned 21 I got my money that I had earned on the farm, $116.00. I gave Mr. Hobday a sketch I had drawn of Dr. Barnardo. In 1943 I started my own business from scratch and thought if I would work as hard for myself as I had been working for someone else I could make it pay. And I did. I have retired now from my business. My wife and I have been back to Old Boy reunions at Watts Naval S chool and we are enjoying life. I have no regrets on being one of Dr. Barnardo's Boys.

John Holman

⸺·⸙⸺

1937

I was sent to Watts Naval Training School in Norfolk. This was a branch of Dr. Barnardo's Homes where about three hundred boys were trained to be sailors, soldiers and bandsmen. The school was a good home but strict, as a matter of fact, I can still feel some of the canes across my hands and buttocks. I also attended Dr. Barnardo's Technical School and from there I was given a medical at Canada House by a Canadian doctor. In June, 1937 I sailed on the Duchess of Bedford with fourteen other Barnardo children.

Bugler Jim Inwards, formerly of Dr. Barnardo's Watts Naval School talks with Gracie Fields. Mr. George Black, Barnardo's last Canadian staff member looks on
— courtesy Jim Inwards

The Watts Naval Training School, Norfolk
— Centennial Museum, Peterborough

We landed at Quebec City and then boarded a train for Toronto where we were met by Mr. and Mrs. John Hobday. We were briefed on the style of life in Canada. One point I remember quite well was that when a farmer speaks, he may seem harsh and not to get upset, this is their way of life. Then Mr. Black, the visiting man, packed all six of us into a taxi. (We took turns breathing!)

I landed at my Canadian farm. I had turned 14 on the way over and felt I was ready for work. My farm family was very good and saw that I got lots to eat and attended Sunday School. Mr. Black came to the farm to see how I was getting on. Then one day I was requested to return to Headquarters, Toronto. When I got there I was introduced to a Mr. Bohemen from Hollywood! He interviewed me on my life at the Watts Naval Academy and I danced the sailor's hornpipe for him. With the information he collected, he thanked me, went back to Hollywood and made a picture called "Lord Jeff". I saw the movie when it came to Canada.

W. W. II broke. I joined the Canadian Navy and was stationed in the Automotive Building, Toronto. I was one of the two youngest sailors to meet Gracie Fields. In 1942 I joined the Canadian Army. Our ship sailed for England. We landed at Liverpool and went into Surrey. While there I found my real family. To this time I did not know any of them but my mother knew of me and even my birthday. On weekends I spent all the time I could with them.

Christmas 1944, I spent with the Army in Rome. I stayed in the army until 1946 and then returned to civilian life.

Back in Canada I went to the Home in Toronto and told them I was finished with the service. I thanked Mr. and Mrs. Hobday and removed the bit of cash I had in my Barnardo Account with the Bank of Commerce. That was the last time I had anything to do with the Barnardo Homes. I do think that the founder Dr. Barnardo was a wonderful person. He stooped to lift up children. He taught us right from wrong and that has stayed with most of us a life time.

Jim Inwards

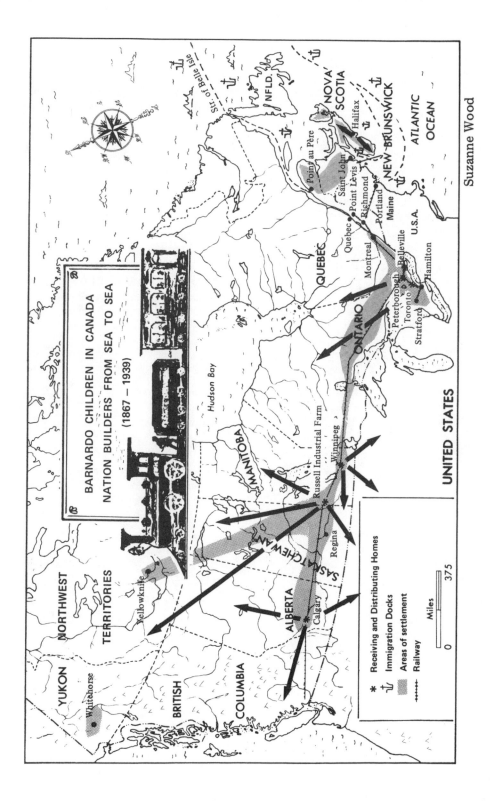

BARNARDO CHILDREN IN CANADA
NATION BUILDERS FROM SEA TO SEA
(1867 – 1939)

Suzanne Wood

* Receiving and Distributing Homes
⚓ Immigration Docks
░ Areas of settlement
········ Railway

Miles
0 ————— 375

APPENDIX

SURVEY OF BARNARDO
IN
CANADA

1868   Jamie Jarvis, first child, emigrated to Canada with Annie MacPherson's Party, Barnardo's first female emigrant followed.

1870   Sprinkling of Barnardo Boys continued to emigrate with Miss Annie MacPherson's emigration parties. Barnardo assists in training programme.

1882   Fifty Barnardo Boys from Stepney Causeway, make up the "Pilgrim Fathers" of Barnardo emigration work into Canada. One hundred Barnardo Boys follow.

1883   First party of 72 Barnardo Girls enter Canada under the care of Miss Emilie Morecroft.

Canadian Agent appointed, A.B. Owen; Canadian Advisory Board formed.

Honourable Senator George A. Cox offers "Hazelbrae", Peterborough to Dr. Barnardo as Canada's first Receiving and Distributing Home.

1912 Renamed the Margaret Cox School for Girls
1929 All Barnardo operations moved to Toronto.

1887   Barnardo travels to Russell, Manitoba, opening site for Industrial Farm For Barnardo Boys. Closed 1904.
Manager Mr. E. A. Struthers Mulock

1889   Barnardo Office and Receiving and Distributing Home for Barnardo Boys opened at Farley Ave., Toronto.

1893   Sir Charles Tupper, Canadian High Commissioner, London encourages Barnardo.

1895   *Ups and Downs,* Canadian Barnardo Publication

1896   Winnipeg Distributing and Receiving Home for Boys and Girls going West. Closed 1918. Manager Mr. E.A.Struthers

1916   Barnardo Emigration to Canada ceases.

1920   First post-war emigration.

1922   New Canadian Headquarters, 538 Jarvis Street, former home of C. Mulock

1926   Prohibition of emigration of children under 14 to Canada

1930   Economic Depression, last supervised Barnardo party.

1939   Final emigration of Barnardo children, 21 boys, 7 girls

1960   Barnardo Office at 466 Briar Hill Avenue, Toronto, closed. All Barnardo records shipped back to England.

BARNARDO EMIGRATION TO CANADA
1867 — 1912

	From 1867-1890	1891	1892	1893	1894	1895	1896	1897	1898	1899	1900	1901
Boys	3038	417	596	758	635	578	490	438	371	446	592	698
Girls	1107	5	131	76	89	155	188	226	242	201	339	315
Total	4145	422	727	834	724	733	678	652	613	647	931	1013

	1902	1903	1904	1905	1906	1907	1908	1909	1910	1911	1912	Total
Boys	684	836	863	981	728	742	630	632	630	591	539	16913
Girls	369	401	403	333	443	340	313	335	332	411	374	7128
Total	1053	1237	1266	1314	1171	1082	943	967	962	1002	913	24041

DOCTOR BARNARDO'S "AFTER SAILING" NOTIFICATION

18 to 26 Stepney Causeway,
London, E.
1888

To _____ (Parent or Guardian) _____

I am desired to inform you that in accordance with the terms of the agreement entered into when

_____ (Name of Child) _____

was received into this Institution, the Managers included her in the party of girls who left these Homes for Canada.

Should you desire to write to her, the address is the

The Secretary, "Dr. Barnardo's Homes, "Hazel-brae, Peterborough, Ontario, Canada. Your letter will need a penny stamp.

Analysis of 1888 Barnardo Emigration Party to Canada

22	were between 6 and 12 years old
67	were over 12.
40	had been in the homes 1 to 3 years
20	under 1 year
29	over 3 years
9	had both parents living
16	had fathers only
36	had mothers only
28	were orphans and some being waif and friendless on admission.
42	came from London
42	from English counties
3	from Ireland
1	from Scotland
1	from Jersey

BARNARDO GIRLS' CANADIAN OUTFIT
— 1898 —

new box

label

key

stationary

brush and comb

haberdashery

handkerchief

Bible

hymn book

2 stuffed dresses (blk/gold)

2 print dresses

2 flanelette n' dresses

2 cotton n' dresses

garters

shoe and boot laces

tooth brush

brush and comb

8 small towels in bag

2 pr. hoses (thick)

2 pr. hoses (thin)

2 flanelette petticoats

1 winter petticoat

1 summer petticoat

2 coarse aprons

2 holland aprons

2 muskin aprons

ulster

tom o'shanter

hat

1 pr. boots

1 pr. oxfords

1 pr. slippers

1 pr. plimsolles

1 pr. gloves

Courtesy — F. Rightmeyer

BARNARDO BOYS' CANADIAN OUTFIT
— 1930 —

1 peaked cap

1 suit

1 pr. rubber soled boots

1 pr. slippers

2 long nightshirts

2 pr. woollen socks

1 pr. overalls

1 set light underwear

2 shirts

2 pocket handkerchiefs

1 pr. braces and one belt

1 ball of wool for sock repairs, needles and thread, boot brush

1Bible

1 marked New Testament

1 Travellers Guide

1 Pilgrims Progress

Courtesy — W. A. Eyden

CHRONOLOGY OF BARNARDO HOMES IN CANADA
1883 - 1963

A. PETERBOROUGH

1883   Hazelbrae donated by Mayor Geo. A. Cox to receive Barnardo Boys and Girls as well as local orphans

1889   Hazelbrae renamed Dr. Barnardo's Home For Girls

1912   Dr. Barnardo's Home in Peterborough renamed in honour of Honourable Senator Geo. A. Cox's deceased wife, The Margaret Cox Home For Girls

1918   Barnardo's London receives deed for Barnardo House and property

1922   Dr. Barnardo's Home, Peterborough closed.

N.B. Marchmont Home, Belleville (Annie MacPherson) amalgamated with Barnardo's, 1925.

B. WINNIPEG AND RUSSELL

E. A. Struthers, Manager

1887-1908   Industrial Farm, Russell, Manitoba.

1897-1906   Receiving and Distributing Home, 115 Pacific Ave., Winnipeg.

1910-1918   Western Headquarters, "Oakwood", 75 Bannerman Ave.

C. TORONTO

1889-1908   Boys Home, Receiving and Distributing, 214 Farley Ave., A. B. Owen, Manager

1909-1922   50-52 Peter Street

1922-1945   538 Jarvis (formerly C. Mulock's estate) Canadian Headquarters for both boys and girls. J.W. Hobday and Rose Hobday, Managers

1946-1950   534 Jarvis St., George Black, Manager.

1948-1952   20 Spadina

1963   Office, 466 Briar Hill Ave., Toronto.

BARNARDO HOMESTEADING EXPENSES — 1896

FIRST EXPENSES

Transportation to Russell	$ 30.00
Expenses of Entry	11.00
Provisions for One Month	15.00
One Yoke Oxen	120.00
Plough	16.00
Repairs	3.00
Cart	25.00
Harness	14.00
House and Stable	66.00
General Household Outfit	25.00
	$325.00

TO BE MET BY:
        Amount of Deposit $150.00
        Advance   175 .00 $325.00
                                        $325.00 $325.00

SUBSEQUENT EXPENSES

Expenses while Backsetting, Repairs, Contingencies, etc.	$ 30.00
Clothing, etc.	25.00
Wintering Oxen	10.00
Seed	25.00
Additional Furniture,etc.	25.00
Provisions,Six Months,Two People	96.00
Harrows	16.00
Plough	16.00
Cow	32.00
	$275.00

TO BE MET BY:
        Six Month's Work with
        team on Farm Home after
        Completing One Month's
        breaking on Homestead. $150.00
Further Advance   125.00 $275.00
                                        $600.00 $600.00

GENEALOGICAL SEARCH

1. Over thirty thousand Barnardo Children were emigrated to Canada between 1882 and 1939. Descendents wishing to secure information about a Barnardo forebearer should address their inquiry to:

    > Dr. Barnardo's,
    > After Care Section,
    > Tanners Lane,
    > Barkingside,
    > Ilford,
    > Essex 1G6 I0G
    > England.

    Enquirers should provide the Barnardo Archives with as much background information as possible: full name, dates, name of ship, sailing date etc. Presently, no specific charge is made for this geneological search but donations towards the Barnardo work would be acceptable.

2. Barnardo emigrants and their descendents are eligible to receive the official Barnardo publication the *Guild Messenger.* This fills the information gap left by the termination of the Canadian *Ups and Downs.* Through the *Guild Messenger* Canadians are able to contact other emigrants and their descendents who came to Canada under Dr. Barnardo's auspices.

3. GENEALOGICAL SOCIETY,
    Box 66, Station Q, Toronto, Ontario, Canada. M4T 2L7
    * maintains a reference library and shares techniques for research

4. PUBLIC ARCHIVES, OTTAWA

    Department of Agriculture RG 17, AI-1, 1852-1920 general correspondance and reports

    Immigration RG 76, Vol. 51 and 52 file 2209, parts 1-4 (microfilm C-4715 and C-4716)

    (These are but two examples of numerous references to Barnardo Children)

Dr. Barnardo's annual lists "Boys Canada Party", Public Archives.

Film No.	Item No.	Dates	Date to be opened
1585	20	Aug. & Oct. 1893	1987
1588	21	March 1894	1989
1589	22	June 1894	1990
1590	23	Aug. & Nov. 1894	1990
1591	24	March 1895	1991
1592	25	June 1895	1991
1595	26	Sept. & Oct. 1895	1991
1596	27	April 1896	1990
1597	28	July & Oct. 1896	1991
1599	29	March, June 1897	1993
1600	30	July & Sept. 1897	1990
1601	31	March 1898	1990
1602	32	July 1898	1992
1603	33	March 1899	1993
	34	July 1899	
1604	35	Sept. 1899	1993
1605	36	March 1900	1996
1607	37	July 1900	1996
1608	38	Sept. 1900	1995
1609	39	March 1901	1996
1610	40	July 1901	1997
1612	41	Sept. 1901	1996
1625	49	July 1904	1998
1626	50	Sept. & Oct. 1904	1998
1634	51	March 1905	1998
1635	52	June 1905	2000
1636	53	Aug. 1905	2001
1637	54	Sept. 1905	2000
1642	55	March 1906	2000
1643	56	May 1906	1999
1644	57	Aug. 1906	2001
1645	58	Oct. 1906	2000
1646	59	Feb. 1907	2002
1655	60	April 1907	2001
	61	July 1907	2002
1656	62	Sept. 1907	2002
	63	March 1908	2002

1663	64	May 1908	2003
	65	July 1908	2003
1669	66	Oct. 1908	2002
1670	67	Feb. 1909	2003
1671	68	May 1909	2003
1672	69	July & Oct. 1909	2004
1673	70	March 1910	2004
1674	71	May, July 1910	2004
	72	Oct. 1910	2004
1675	73	Feb. 1911	2005
1676	74	June 1911	2005

Select Bibliography

Acton, Janice. *Women at Work*. Women Press Toronto, 1974.

Barnardo, T.J. *Something Attempted, Something Gained*. London, 1889.

Barnardo, S.L. and Marchant, James. *Memoirs of the Late Dr. Barnardo*. London: Hodder and Stoughton, 1907.

Bagnell, Ken. *The Little Immigrants*. Macmillan, 1980.

Batt, John H. *Dr. Barnardo, Foster Father of Nobody's Children*. London, S. W. Partridge, 1904.

Berton, Pierre. *The Last Spike*. McClelland and Stewart, 1971.

Bliss, Michael. *Sir Joseph Flavelle*. University of Toronto Press, 1978.

Bready, J. Wesley. *Dr. Barnardo, Physician, Pioneer, Prophet*. London, Allen and Unwin, 1930.

Bunyan, John. *Pilgrim's Progress*.

Cardinal, Roger. *Outsider Art*. Praeger, 1972.

Harrison, Phyllis. *The Home Children*. Winnipeg, Watson & Dwyer Publishing, 1979.

Hocking, Silas. *Her Benny*. Gallery Press, 1968.

Irwin, Grace. *The Seventh Earl*. Erdmans, 1976.

Magnuson, J. and Petrie, D. *Orphan Train*. Fawcett, 1978.

Mayhew, Henry. *London Labour and the London Poor*. Dover, 1968.

Morton, W.L. *Manitoba, A History*. Toronto, University of Toronto Press, 1967.

Neuman, A.R. *Dr. Barnardo*. London.

Parr, Joy. *Labouring Children*. London, 1980. Croom Helm.

Pinchbeck, Ivy and Hewitt, Margaret. *Children in English Society,* 2 vols. London, Routledge & Kegan Paul, 1973.

Scott, Carolyn. *Ever Open Door.* Lutterworth, 1972.

Strickland, Sam. *Twenty-Years in Canada West.* 1853.

Suggitt, Gladys. *Roses and Thorns.* Fenelon Falls, 1972.

Sutherland, Neil. *Children in English-Canadian Society.* Toronto, University of Toronto Press, 1976.

Thompson, A.E. *Jarvis Street* Personal Library, 1980.

Wagner, Gillian. *Barnardo.* London, Weidenfeld ands Nicolson, 1979.

Wallis, H.M. *Ontario History,* James Wallis, Dec. 1961 — Article

Wymer, Norman. *Father of Nobody's Children.* London, Hutchinson and Co., 1954.

INDEX

Admissions 19
Adoption 37, 57
After-sailing Notices 123
Agricultural Hall 15
Allan Line 33, 46
Analysis of Party 123
Annesley, Capt. & Mrs. 46
Assineboine River 68

Bank Accounts 55
Bank of Commerce 55
Bannerman Ave. Winnipeg 76
Barnardo Outfit 29, 93, 124
Barnardo Special 35, 45, 91
Barnardo, Thomas John 14, 67
Belle Isle 34
Belleville, Ont. 45
Bethune, Rev. 23
Black, George 64, 116
Blake, S. H. 40
Bradburn Opera House 46
Bread Basket 67
Burnham, John 47

Cairns, Earl 40
Canada Clause 31
Canada List 29
Children's Friend Society 23
Cholera 15
Christmas 50, 81, 93
Chronological Summeries 125
Cobourg Star 23
Colonization Scheme 72
"Corinthian" 33
Cox, George A. 39, 40, 46
Custody 31

Death Rate 57
Dominion Illustrated 70
Doyle, Andrew 24, 57
Dublin, Ireland 14

Elkhorn, Manitoba 73
Elmslie, Syrie Louise 16
Emigration Principles 26
Evangelistic Revival 14
Ever-Open Door 20
Export Emporium 18

Fielder, Frederick 25, 40
Fields, Gracie 117
Fleming, Sir Sandford 40
Flavelle, Joseph 40, 46

Garden Hill, Ont. 93
Genealogical Search 127
Girls' Garden Village 42, 48, 82
Globe, The (Toronto) 56
Grand Trunk Railway 36, 40
Guild Messenger 56

Haultain, General 41
Hazelbrae 40, 41, 46, 48
Hobday, Rose & John 34, 97, 100
Homesteading 126

Industrial Farm 68
Infant Colony 56
Insure Children 86

Jarvis, Jamie 25
Jarvis Street 48, 83, 106
Jersey, Isle of 17, 111

Kennedy, Miss Jennie 2

Labour House 17
Landing Card 32
Litigation 31
Liverpool 101
London, Eng. 47, 69
Lorne, Lord 65, 67

MacPherson, Annie 25
Maine 35
"Melita" 31
Merino 41
Midland Railway 39
Montreal 80
Moodie, Susanna 37
Morecroft, Emilie 39
Motto 16, 20
Mulock, Sir William 49, 67

New Brunswick 35
Nights and Days 42
Nova Scotia 35

Owen, Alfred de Brissac 35, 42, 80

Pacific Ave., Winnipeg 73
"Parisian" 33
Peterborough, Ont. 40
Peterborough Examiner 41, 47, 49
Pilgrims' Progress 39
Point au Père 35
Point Levis 35, 45
"Polynesian" 46
Poor Law Act 31

Quebec 45, 61

Ragged Schools 15
Rebellions 23
Robinson, Peter 23
Russell, Manitoba 67, 69
Rye, Maria 24

Sanderson, Millie 42
"Sardinia" 33
Saskatchewan 76
Shaftsbury, Earl of 16
Shaw, George Bernard 19
"Sicilian" 82
Socket, The Rev. Thomas 23
Stanley, Lord 70
Stent, Margaret 48
Stephen, Lord Mount 61
Stepney Causeway 28, 79
Strathcona, Lord 61
Strickland, Col. Samuel 23
Struthers, E.A. 69, 76

Toronto 83, 90
Traill, Catharine Parr 23
"Tunisian" 33
Tupper, Sir Charles 61, 67

Ups and Downs 31, 51

Virden Advance 75
Visitation 55

Wallis 40, 41
War 61
Watts Naval School 116
Whitla, R.J. 75
Widows 19
Winnipeg, Man. 75, 76
Woodgate, Miss 48